GOOGLE ME

MEANING SYSTEMS

GOOGLE ME

ONE-CLICK DEMOCRACY

BARBARA CASSIN

Translated by MICHAEL SYROTINSKI

Fordham University Press   *New York 2018*

This book was originally published in French as Barbara Cassin, *Google-moi: La
deuxième mission de l'Amérique*, Copyright © Éditions Albin Michel, 2007.

Cet ouvrage, publié dans le cadre d'un programme d'aide à la publication, bénéficie
de la participation de la Mission Culturelle et Universitaire Française aux Etats-Unis,
service de l'Ambassade de France aux EU.

This work, published as part of a program of aid for publication, received support
from the Mission Culturelle et Universitaire Française aux Etats-Unis, a department of
the French Embassy in the United States.

Fordham University Press has no responsibility for the persistence or accuracy of
URLs for external or third-party Internet websites referred to in this publication and
does not guarantee that any content on such websites is, or will remain, accurate or
appropriate.

Fordham University Press also publishes its books in a variety of electronic formats.
Some content that appears in print may not be available in electronic books.

Visit us online at www.fordhampress.com.

Library of Congress Cataloging-in-Publication Data available online at http://catalog
.loc.gov.

Printed and bound in Great Britain by Marston Book Services Ltd, Oxfordshire

20 19 18   5 4 3 2 1

First edition

CONTENTS

TRANSLATOR'S PREFACE

The following text is a translation of Barbara Cassin's critique of Google, *Google-moi: La deuxième mission de l'Amérique*, first published in French by Albin Michel in 2007. There were other more familiar, often journalistic accounts of Google published around the same time, such as John Battelle's *The Search* and David Vise's *The Google Story*, both of which Cassin references, or more recent volumes by media theorists, such as Siva Vaidhyanathan's *The Googlization of Everything* (2011), or Steven Levy's *In the Plex: How Google Thinks, Works, and Shapes Our Lives* (2011), or even Eric Schmidt and Johathan Rosenberg's own recent *How Google Works*. But Cassin's book is the first to embed a critique of Google into a philosophical genealogy. What makes this book such a unique perspective on the phenomenon of Google and Internet culture more generally is that Cassin brings to bear an extraordinary philosophical rigor and sophistication to her account of the rise of Google and the impact it has had on cultural activities worldwide, most crucially on the forms that knowledge takes. Cassin is a formidable Hellenist by training, although her work overturns much of what we thought we understood about Greek philosophy, unsettling conventional wisdom or subverting critical commonplaces, and celebrating, for example, the Sophists over and against Plato's philosopher-kings. In *Google Me*, her deep knowledge of Greek culture, philology, and philosophy (and of the history of philosophy and thought more broadly) becomes the lens through which she challenges the

political and ethical basis on which Google makes its claims and the
manner in which it carries out its operations.

Her critique is thus a serious one, and one we would all be well
advised to take seriously, since it goes to the heart of what we often
think of uncritically as the benefits that accrue to humanity from
increasingly advanced Internet technology. The book starts out as
a very readable and entertaining historical (and personal) account,
but it is really in the later chapters that the philosophical stakes become clear. As her argument gathers pace, she will by turns marshal
Heidegger's thinking on technology, Spinoza's concept of monads,
Deleuze's notion of multitude, Hannah Arendt's ideas about language and translation, and the distinction between morality and
ethics in Kant, as well as anchoring her discussion in Plato and the
Sophists. Cassin takes Google to task for its self-proclaimed "mission" to democratize information, and for imposing its *doxa* as
truth. *Doxa* (opinion, although its polysemy is considerably richer,
as Cassin explains) has a long history in Greek philosophy, de-
nounced by Plato, for example, as secondhand or received wisdom
rather than the epistemologically verifiable truth of "what is." Indeed, what is characterized as "doxography" becomes a dramatic
staging of the tensions between *doxa* and *aletheia* (truth) that
structure the early Sophistic dialogues, and which allow for Cassin's
highly original analysis of the ontological status of "information" in
today's hypertechnologized world. This exploitation of the potential of *doxa* as a theoretical paradigm can also be seen in Cassin's
more recent works, such as *Sophistical Practice: Towards a Consistent Relativism*, or her reading of Lacanian psychoanalysis as itself
an essentially sophistical practice, *Jacques le Sophiste: Lacan, logos
et psychoanalyse.*[1]

The almost breathless pace at which the power and sophistication of search engines and of information technology in general
have evolved since this book was first published naturally mean that
its frame of reference, and its political and cultural contexts—most
notably the compelling analogy between American foreign policy

in the immediate aftermath of 9/11, the self-righteous "war against evil," and Google's own "global" mission—can now be read with the hindsight of recent political and technological developments. Google has of course continued to consolidate its dominant position at the heart of the Internet and of search engine technology, and the creeping Google-dependency Cassin warns of in *Google Me* is now all-pervasive. Who among us does not on an almost daily basis use Google Books, Google Images, YouTube (owned by Google), Google Maps, Google Earth, Google Scholar, and Google Translate, not to mention the increasing array of Google apps, Google's Chrome browser, Gmail, cloud computing, or Google phones? Other technological developments that were new in 2007 we now take for granted, such as e-books, and the ever-more sophisticated Kindles or other e-readers, and despite its promise to shift the global center of gravity, the European search engine Quaero was simply unable to compete with Google's power, so the prospect of a European rival remains as distant as ever. That said, the United States relinquished its control over domain names in September 2015, so changes, for example, to the .fr extension can be made without the approval of the US authorities in what could be seen as a first step toward a multiactor, global Internet governance framework.

At the same time, the whole question of the relationship between communications technology, mass surveillance programs, and democratic freedom has been thrown into dramatic relief by the very high-profile cases of Julian Assange, the founder of WikiLeaks, which made publicly available mass data from previously secret or classified US government intelligence files, and of Edward Snowden, the former National Security Agency employee and whistleblower, who revealed to the world the extraordinary scale of mass surveillance programs and covert hacking operations that are being carried out in the name of "global security."

Although we are dealing, then, with a constantly shifting and ever more complex landscape, the developments we have witnessed

xii   TRANSLATOR'S PREFACE

over the last few years have demonstrated all the more forcefully the insight and prescience of Cassin's analysis of the claims made by Google and the cultural, political, economic, and juridical implications one could extrapolate if its "mission" were to succeed. *Google Me* thus remains utterly relevant to us today, precisely because it situates what is ultimately a culturally and politically specific moment in the recent history of information technology within a far larger historical and philosophical framework. Indeed, one of the core arguments of the book is to show how the concepts and language Google uses to define its mission come out of a long and often complex philosophical prehistory.

A number of Cassin's insistent themes and preoccupations in this book can be seen in other works she has published, both prior to the original French edition of *Google-moi* and subsequently. Perhaps the most important and best known of these is the monumental *Dictionary of Untranslatables: A Philosophical Lexicon.*[2] This is a quasi-encyclopedic compendium of key terms in the history of philosophy, each presented as a philologically and philosophically rich study of transformations through translation between languages and cultures. These are all terms that have had a deep and long-lasting impact on thinking across the humanities, and the *Dictionary of Untranslatables* is thus a volume unlike any other in the history of philosophy, in that it considers concepts not just as words but also as words that enter into all sorts of problematic exchanges with other words in other languages, in a kind of vast multilingual performance that Cassin calls *"philosopher en langues"* ("philosophizing in languages," with the accent emphatically on the plural). Cassin herself provides a useful nutshell-definition of "untranslatable" in her preface, where she writes "To speak of *untranslatables* in no way implies that the terms in question, or the expressions, the syntactical or grammatical turns, are not and cannot be translated: the untranslatable is rather what one keeps on (not) translating [*l'intraduisible, c'est plutôt ce qu'on ne cesse pas de (ne pas) traduire*]." "Untranslatable" is thus about not the failure of translation but the endlessly productive energy of those points of resistance to translation.

One feature the *Dictionary of Untranslatables* uses to great effect is the *encadré*, or dialog box, a kind of sideways explanatory note embedded within the text that explores in greater depth one or more aspect of a given entry. Cassin makes further use of this box in *Google Me*. More than simply providing an editorial template, however, it is the intellectual project that the *Dictionary of Untranslatables* represents, as well as its subsequent translations into other languages, which underpins the critique of Google, bound up as it is with a certain cultural and thus linguistic imperialism. The question of translation indeed comes to the fore in the latter half of *Google Me*, and Cassin argues passionately for the multiplicity and diversity of languages (including within each language and cultural tradition), over and against the linguistic (and, more important, *philosophical*) impoverishment of "Globish," or Global English. Finally, *Google Me* demonstrates its contemporary relevance in showing how the borders between search and research have become increasingly blurred. This is ever truer nowadays with the imperative to publish more and more online, through open access, and because of the consequent ease with which one can now conduct and publish research. Google Books and Google Scholar are naturally a boon to students and researchers, but Cassin argues that the economic and commercial interests underlying Google's many "services" fundamentally compromise any principled claim to democracy or universality. When this principle is extended to research evaluation, in which we have to contend with the increasing prevalence of quantifiable metrics (citation indices, journal impact factors, article download counts, etc.) as tools to assess research quality, as well as the use of global ranking lists whose methodology mirrors Google's own PageRank search results, it is hardly surprising that we are in danger of becoming, in Hannah Arendt's words, "cultured philistines." Just as with Google and PageRank, quality has become an emergent property of quantity. Indeed, this is the subject of one of Cassin's most recent polemical interventions in the politics and philosophy of education, *Derrière les grilles: Sortons du tout-évaluation*,[3] where the French word *grilles* refers both to imprisonment ("behind bars") and to the grids into which we all have to fit accounts of our activity for the purposes of systematic evaluation.

The present translation has had to resolve a number of tricky problems, notably in shifting the center of gravity of the target readership from a principally French or European one to an Anglophone American one. Given Cassin's sustained and profound investment in questions of translation, I felt it was important to keep that dimension of the book very much to the fore, particularly in the witty, sometimes mischievous (and often deliberately untranslatable) multilingual wordplay, or with the kinds of experiments she performs, with Google Translate, for example, or in her reading of different attempts to translate James Joyce into French. A number of footnotes explaining cultural references that would be familiar to French readers are intended to be informative without being overly intrusive or interventionist. A few other notes serve as factual updates where I thought it would be helpful. Finally, I have tried throughout to retain Cassin's punchy and provocative style, which is quite deliberately intended as a punctual intervention at a given point in time. This is not only a book written by a French philosopher whose perspective on culture, language, and American imperialism marks it out from those more familiar to Anglo-American readers, but it is also at the same time a very personal account, as a subject/object caught in Google's Web, and a kind of playful, performative experiment, that in its very performance powerfully deconstructs the immediacy the Web *purports* to offer.

Michael Syrotinski

PREFACE TO THE ENGLISH-LANGUAGE EDITION

Barbara Cassin

I am very surprised that this book, *Google Me*, should find its place in the United States now. Only now, and not ten years ago, in 2007, when it was first published in France, but precisely now that Google/Alphabet has swallowed up so many companies.

In order to be readable, my account needs to be situated within an alternative temporality, analogous (if you will pardon the grand claim) to the one Nietzsche invoked in his *Unzeitgemässe Betrachtungen* (*Untimely Meditations*); an untimely time, in short, a philosophical time.

In order to avoid it simply being out of season, or out of date or fashion, Michael Syrotinski, my translator and collaborator, has updated the salient facts with his indispensable translator's notes and in his introduction has sketched out the elements of the new context.

By way of lending it a more contemporary relevance, however, I will add one further consideration that is close to my heart and that should bring about a broader collaboration, for which I have not found the right interlocutors in France, to my immense regret. This is the transformation of the relationship to translation.

In 2004, I published the *Vocabulaire européen des philosophies: Dictionnaire des intraduisibles*, which explores, with French as a "metalanguage," a certain number of symptoms of differences, both semantic and syntactic, between some fifteen primarily European languages within the domain of philosophy, understood very broadly as a porous and invasive discipline. I called these symptoms "untranslatables," by which I meant not that which is not translated but that which one never stops (not) translating, from the words we use to greet one another and open up a world (*Salaam* or *Shalom*, for example, mean something quite different from *Hello* or *Good morning*), to the difference between Mind, *Geist*, and *Esprit*, different sets of terms par excellence. This improbable work has now been translated or is being translated or adapted into nearly a dozen languages.

In the latter half of 2016, I curated an exhibition in a major French museum, the MuCEM in Marseille, entitled "Après Babel, Traduire" (After Babel, Translate), in which I have tried to show how translation informs our languages and civilizations, and especially how it constitutes a know-how with differences, and one so expert that in my view it offers the best model for the humanities we need. If we are going to think through what the "Digital Humanities" mean, this is what we have to put to work.

Returning to Google, and to Google Translate: When I wrote *Google-moi*, I performed an experiment that I can no longer perform today, and that I talk about in the book.[1] I am in fact very happy *not* to be able to do it again: If I enter the sentence from the Bible "And God created man in his image" into Google Translate in French, English, and German, the translation I get in French, English, and German is now correct, coherent, and consistent (it no longer makes us laugh at the incredible truth it produced back then: that man created God in his image). At the same time as the translation of semantics, the translation of syntax and word order has made immense progress. The reason for this is that the technology and the very idea behind computer-assisted translation have undergone a fundamental change. We no longer go, as with the first Wordnet, from one language to another via the oh so poorly disambiguated pivot language of English, but directly from a word cloud contextualized in one language to a word cloud contextualized in another language. Now, these word clouds are precisely what

preoccupy us in the *Dictionary of Untranslatables*. This is what I
wanted to have on the cover of the original French volume, to pay
homage to the great, late nineteenth-century German linguist and
diplomat Wilhelm von Humboldt, who in my opinion sketched out
the very space and project of our *Dictionary*: "a most seductive
work" that would, he writes, study the "synonymy of languages."[2]

With this recent evolution of the very framework of computer-
assisted translation, quantity of contexts is always a necessary pre-
requisite of the quality of the connections being made. But now
quality is, for good and without irony, an emergent property of
quantity, since for the computer-assisted translator conceived in
this way, just as for a clinical medical practitioner, there will only be
cases. Performance, just like clinical practice or other kinds of jobs,
is linked to the number of cases treated each as it comes, far from
the protocol of any diagnostic and statistical manual that one fills
out by ticking boxes, and whose primary effect, as most of us know,
is the "ritalinization" of those of our children who are not already
slouched in front of the TV. We need to think in terms of cases and
symptoms to respect the singularity of idioms as much as of individuals. In a sense, what I am fervently calling for here—for which
I tried unsuccessfully to secure a collaboration with Google Translate in this exhibition on translation—is a new way of qualifying
quantity, by combining numbers with an analysis of symptoms. I am
unable to say more precisely what I mean by this, but I know that I
want to point the way toward a possible complementarity between
the poetry of symptoms and the intoxication of large numbers, in
order to rethink computer-assisted translation and go beyond "linguistic flavors."

Is there anything else really new?

More than ever, Google has now become a magic tool that we
all use every day, with the near disappearance of any digital dis-
sonance—today, broadly speaking, whenever we eat we are connected. . . . Google's ecosystem functions as an infrastructure of the
Internet. We all know the dangers of this dominant position and of

the rule of "everything," which not only threaten our privacy but indeed power and politics as such, whose supremacy (Aristotle said of politics that it was "architectonic") can be undermined, at least locally, by a power like that of Google. During my most recent visits to China, one of the computer "geeks" among my students came every morning to remove the "night barriers," the obstacles preventing me from having access to Gmail and to Google. Google as a countervailing power above the law, starting with tax laws: more or less all the world's information, for better and for worse.

Google's two mottos, which I followed as the threads of my argument, also remain unchanged: "Organize all the world's information" and "Don't be evil" are more present than ever. At JFK Airport, I picked up from a big pile a copy of *How Google Works*,[3] by Eric Schmidt and Jonathan Rosenberg (with Alan Eagle, and with a foreword by Larry Page—they are all there). "Don't be evil" is a subheading in the chapter "Believe your own slogans": "That is the power of a great culture. It can make each member of the company better. And it can make the company ascendant" (65). There is, or was, in France a satirical television show that we (who are "we"?) all liked a lot, *Les Guignols de l'Info*. The Sylvester Stallone puppet, with his briefcase, suit, and tie, was always basically saying just that, or more precisely, "global capitalism" is always basically saying just that. No surprise, then, that in this respect nothing has changed, even if everything is hardening from one crisis to the next, from one failure to the next, or from refugees to those who are drowning in the graveyard of Europe that the Mediterranean has turned into.

Is there really nothing new?

In fact there is.

The main emphasis of technology has shifted considerably.

Ten years ago, nothing mattered more than being ranked by Google. Nowadays, what matters is the number of *likes*, the way in which you *reach out* or *share*—I use the English terms even though I am writing in French, since English is, of all the world languages, the native tongue of this connected community. Perhaps it would be more appropriate now to write not a *Google Me*, but a *Like Me*! The triumph of social media, particularly Facebook, foregrounds other values and other forms of interaction, such that Google, with its core work ethic, seems to my younger interlocutors more like a respectable IT company, slightly outmoded or out of date, however well it performs, including financially. What matters are no longer algorithms but immediate visibility, shared without outside intervention, weighting, or mediation, and classified solely according to what is going on around us, as on Twitter or Instagram. With the instantaneousness of the "I" who "posts"—so no longer a question of "you are the Web," but of "I" am the Web—it is all about sharing emotions, and having what is intuitive be wholly visible, in an absolute blurring of the private/public distinction, but for the benefit of a privacy that redefines the borders of the public by defining itself as "social."

When seen through the lens of social networks, the Google Guys now look more like white-collar workers. Google has become "hardware," and Google+ has simply failed. "Ask the hardest questions," which is precisely what Eric Schmidt and Jonathan Rosenberg do, by ending *How Google Works* with a question: "Could the social web make search obsolete?" (49).

Yes. Certainly, if not obsolete, at least perfectly trivial, and reframed within its own limits.

So where does this leave Google? It is simple, it seems to me. Google turned Alphabet (with the emphasis on "bet"), with a single letterbox in Delaware, is the next move.

With connected objects, first of all: Google's glasses have been something of a flop, but who among us does not dream of sleeping while driving, and of being transported in an automobile, which truly is an "auto-mobile," as if on a flying carpet? The money to be spent and to be made is certainly there, in considerable amounts.

At the same time there is augmented humanity, which is *the* burning topic nowadays. Connected objects are beginning to augment this "humanity," which we will perhaps no longer be in much of a position to define exactly, for a time at least, nor to say what we would want it to look like. As far as genomes and gene therapy go, things are proceeding well; we are soon going to be able to treat some illnesses quite differently, and even to prevent them. But what of the "dark side of the force"?

Here the questions of translation and of augmented humanity converge. About five years ago "Google Brain," whose very name implies a radical confusion between nature and culture, ushered in a new age of machine translation, no longer based on number and statistics but on neural networks. Artificial Intelligence (AI) refers not only to the intelligence of robots or translating machines, but also that of people who are connected, self-repairing, and soon to be as durable as quasi-immortal machines. The talk is of "The Great AI Awakening"—not America First, but AI First.[4]

So does Artificial Intelligence change something about our forms of knowledge or our representation of consciousness? Certainly it does. Does it mean a considerable improvement in machine translation? Certainly it does. But when we say that a machine "learns," we need to remember that it only ever learns what its creator has given it the possibility of learning, even if everything makes it seem "as if" it is learning all by itself—as if. How else does a child learn, or more precisely, how else does a child behave, from a behaviorist point of view? Might we believe that a child learns like a machine that is structured like a neural network and that a machine learns like an augmented human being?

At what point can we say there is a moment of disruption, invention, autonomy, and no longer just a qualitative leap based on quantity? Strictly speaking, there is no hesitation in knowing who is the master, which of machine and man is "the Brain." Yet, since man and the object he produces are simultaneously coaugmented, it is becoming more and more difficult from the outside to distinguish between on the one hand the master and the model and on the other hand the product. As Borges says of translation, in his own paradoxical and subtle way, "the original is unfaithful to the translation."[5]

The extent to which we need a "Don't be evil"—which I absolutely don't believe in, and which no authority is in a position to guarantee—terrifies me. We have the choice between Protagoras ("Man is the measure of all things"), Plato's *Laws* ("God is the measure of all things"), and Aristotle's *Ethics*, from which we deduce that money is the measure of all things.[6] Until we have proof to the contrary, money, in the sense of money to be made, indeed seems to be the interpretation that has the firmest grip on what remains of the real when we are dealing with Google.

"Some would find this chilling. We find this inspiring." As usual ("As usual," "Comme d'habitude," is the title of the famous French song that was translated into English as "My Way"), it is the "we" that worries me, and that I find most concerning.

GOOGLE ME

INTRODUCTION: WHY BE INTERESTED IN GOOGLE?

ANECDOTES-SYMPTOMS

Why am I interested in Google, and why is anyone interested in Google? For me, it all started with two anecdotes.

"Barbara Cassin"?

"Hello, I know who you are. I Googled you." This is how one Internet-savvy stranger greeted me in his car one day as he was about to drive me to see friends we had in common. There are three "Barbara Cassins" I know of to date, including a lieutenant commander who is a spokesperson for the New Zealand navy and an American ophthalmologist. As Lacan explains in one of his major interventions from the early 1970s, "a language, among others, is nothing more than the integral of equivocations its history leaves in it."[1] In this case a woman, among other women, is nothing more than the sum of the equivocations her name has Googled.

But, then, who apart from her and those close to her knows that there is any equivocation? Nothing indicates or proves it, especially since a hit at *Who's Who* asking you to pay six euros for an individual biography of Barbara Cassin produces the same entry for all three Barbara Cassins. "Barbara Cassin ophthalmologist USA" will have my life, since *Who's Who* has bought the name that "I" bear, and online booksellers list the *Dictionary of Untranslatables*, the *Dictionary of Eye Terminology*, and *Seeing* (!) *Helen in Every Woman* side by side.[2] All anyone knows is that "Barbara Cassin"—that's me—spoke last September at the Supreme Court in Johannesburg at a conference with Albie Sachs on the repercussions of the Truth and Reconciliation Commission, and on September 14 she—this time the woman from New Zealand—took part in a conference on "Investigation and Prosecution Of Cases of Child Abuse—With Deaf/Hard of Hearing Victims and Witnesses" sponsored by the Department of Children and Families at the Riverview Hospital, Connecticut. This is consistent enough when you add it up; "I" would agree more or less with all of my selves.

The Two Banner Sentences

At a colloquium in Thessalonica in the spring of 2005, a representative of Google Europe presented the plan for a digital library, Google Books, as he stood across from Jean-Marie Borzeix, who was there on behalf of the National Library of France, and the European Digital Library. *"Our mission is to organize all the information in the world"*—a sentence only one of the two could utter, and I am very pleased about that. This is the sentence that is now at the top of Google's homepages, with, as an added value, the goal of making it freely available to all: "Google's mission is to organize the world's information and make it universally accessible and useful," a goal that an article in *Le Monde* from December 29, 2005, called "quasi-philosophical."

This mission statement is hard to digest. It frightens me—indeed I cannot understand how displaying it and making sense of it would not frighten anyone. When I then notice in the next sentence that the company's second "motto" ("be *corporate*," young IT professionals are told) is "Don't be evil," my fear is mixed with disgust at this use of an ethical claim, however unsurprising it may be. These two sentences are the guiding thread at the core of this book, and I would like to work through the implications of each word, and how they are articulated in a language. I will work through them neither as an IT professional nor as a politician but as a philosopher.

RELEVANCE TO THE PRESENT DAY
AND FUNDAMENTAL QUESTIONS
Pastism/Presentism

Web tourism and popular sentiment are two components of the question that are hard to digest and difficult to escape, but the biggest risk is "philosophical": How can we negotiate between Heidegger's reactionary yet lucid anathema to the essence of technics, and the glorification of globalized "presentism," which gambles on technology improving the condition of everyone in the world? Yet the question has to be confronted: We (who are we?) will no longer live without the Internet and something like Google, so how do we live best, or for the best, with it?

We could thus not be further from *philosophia perennis*, eternal philosophy, since we have to deal with too many immediate problems, caught in their temporal flow. Everything changes from one day to the next, and there is a constant stream of new announcements: Quaero,[3] the European Digital Library, the evolution of author rights and copyright being debated in Parliament, changes to the Centre National de Recherches Scientifiques (CNRS) to align it with the roles of national agencies (for Research, for Innovation), and the establishment of a large number of competitive laboratories, modeled on European structures that have already become mammoth-like and anglicized down to their use of a kind of Global English, or "Globish," with everything always already e-structured (*knowledge-based society*, the idiom of keywords, with *peer review* and *citation indices* in the place of serious evaluation), built-in obsolescence and opportunism, with short term following on the heels of long term.[4]

Google/The Internet

What is more, we must not confuse Google and the Internet, even if Google itself encourages us to.

Google is a limited company registered in America, founded in 1998, and floated on the stock exchange in 2004. It is the name of an exceptionally high-performance search engine, developed around 1995 by Sergey Brin and Larry Page, two young doctoral students at Stanford University. This search engine is based on an algorithm called PageRank (because it ranks web pages, but also perhaps because Page was one of its main architects and because humor was part of the culture of the company). It is perhaps not as well known as it should be that this algorithm was the property of Stanford University and was exclusively licensed to Google until 2011.[5] This piece of information is without doubt key to the way Google has evolved: Since 2003, it has become less a search engine than an application platform that is endlessly offering more and more extraordinary new services.

The Internet, for its part, is the worldwide network that enables the whole world to be interconnected.[6] Google does not give access to the Internet, since it is not an Internet service provider, but once one is connected, it enables one to search—Google's primary purpose—and to use the Internet. The spotlight has inevitably fallen on Google since the publication of Jean-Noël Jeanneney's *Google and the Myth of Universal Knowledge*.[7] With Google Books and the ambition it has expressed to digitize all of the books in all of the libraries in the world, starting with five willing Anglo-American libraries, Google was perceived as an attack on "us" and our European culture. The question remained, though, of knowing whether Google was an exception, whose success was so fortunate that it has in effect become unrivaled, or rather the rule, the model that its competitors imitated, and that, moreover, imitates them by taking their ideas and people. Google is, after all, only one of the "big four," along with Microsoft, Yahoo!, and AOL, all of them American, and year after year they propose one merger after another, one agreement after another, one court case after another, increasingly offering the same program and the same range of services.

The "Best" Search Engine

Google, though, has positioned itself as the best, and the two preeminent qualities it presents as distinctive correspond to its two key sentences: organization and goodwill.

Google's main characteristic is its secret algorithm, like a manufacturing secret, that enables it to organize results in a "better" way, and thus to respond better to searches. The features of this algorithm are well known and proudly flaunted, even if the algorithm in its variables is a secret. They are, according to Google, "democratic" and thus support its mission of universality. We have to ask the question, of course: How exactly is Google democratic, and what kind of democracy are we dealing with?

Google is also the "best" in that it wants what is best, and in that its goodwill makes this company a moral being. This goodwill is linked to its second distinctive quality: being able to separate out "pure" search results from advertising, in other words, not allowing the rank of a result, as Yahoo! does for example, to be biased by an advertiser's money, but always clearly demarcating (the) search and advertising, or the links generated by the algorithm and the links generated by the sponsors. Google sometimes calls this the "separation of church and state," or the integrity of Jesus as opposed to the venality of Caesar (unless it is the other way round). This disinterestedness will also have to be examined closely.

Response Strategies

Whatever the case, there is room for at least two kinds of response or riposte to Google's "challenge," and they are not mutually exclusive:

1. a strategic-reactive response, along the lines of Galileo reacting to GPS: Europe needs a search engine that does not depend on a search engine from elsewhere (and how could it bear to be dependent on a "disclaimer" such as the one Google stipulates!),[8] that is, something other than Google, or *allos*.

2. an inventive-active response: We have to do something different altogether, taking as our starting point what Google aims to do but does not have, or is not (at least not yet), and what we want, but that Google cannot give us, in other words, something other than Google, or *heteros*.

Here again, several scenarios are possible. There is nothing to prevent us from imagining a form of competition-based independence, which would mean we are dependent on several elsewheres, in the same way that we depend on several oil, gas, or energy suppliers (India, Japan, and China each have, or will have, their own competitive search engines). There is also nothing to prevent us from imagining sharing data, including of course with Google, a sort of global potlatch of free online data for all people of goodwill, but each time with different kinds of added value, precisely according to other "values" to be added, that are local, and even fragmented and multiple.

The politics and the strategy escape "us," but not without producing two simultaneous impressions. First of all, the impression of being at a point in time when everything is possible, including that of making an impact or having an influence from nowhere in particular, or just from where we happen to be (all points of reference have been put into question so profoundly that any initiative seems to have its place). Second, the impression that everything is happening without "us," that technology is performing us, and deciding on what is possible, or what will be relevant in the future, before we are even aware of it. The threshold of incompetence of the individual has obviously been reached, which is really why society is in such need of good sense.

1

THE INTERNET REVEALED THROUGH GOOGLE

NOT SINCE GUTENBERG

"Not since Gutenberg." These words sound like the opening lines of a modern encyclical: "Not since Gutenberg . . . has any invention empowered individuals and transformed access to information as profoundly as Google."[1] Fair enough to say this of the Internet, but of Google? It is one search engine among others, run by a private company of the same name. But it leads us to think that Google is precisely not "one among others." It is, says David Vise, our *global favorite*, and for millions of users it ends up being the same as the Internet. But it is the Internet, not Google, that produces effects. Google's practice (both in the objective sense—to practice Google—and in the subjective sense of the way Google does things, how it proceeds) is simply an excellent means by which the Internet is made apparent. This is why I would like first of all to explain what the Internet represents for someone of my generation, an intermediate generation for whom the screen and the keyboard came after books—a generation that understands that one might call a mouse a *mulot* [fieldmouse], as Jacques Chirac did in *Les Guignols*.[2] A generation that grew up with handwritten letters, with their instinctive graphology and their polite phrases that were a kind of sociological norm, before email with its informal modes of address. A generation, finally, that spent, or supposedly spent, a long time in libraries, and so marveled at CD-ROMs and electronic corpora in the days before we had broadband.

Google is not the Internet, and neither is it a web browser like Safari or Internet Explorer, even if more and more users set their browser's homepage to Google ("Google became my default right away!").[3] It is a search engine, like Yahoo! and MSN, whose primary mission is to carry out searches on the Internet. The difference of which Google boasts with respect to other search engines is precisely that it has no portal strategy. It does not try to hold your attention as long as possible, with "sticky" content, such as advertising that jumps out at you in pop-up windows; it sends you as quickly as possible somewhere else, toward the pages that you are searching for without knowing them. If a "portal strategy tries to own all of the information," Page says, Google is "happy to send you to the other sites. In fact, that's the point."[4] This is, moreover, one of Google's angelic arguments in its legal battles. When Agence France Presse (AFP) attacked it for making the commercial property of its photographs freely available, Google replied that it directed more customers toward them than it took away from them, and that Reuters, unlike AFP, had the good grace to be pleased about it. This was how the notion was born that Google coincides with the Internet.[5]

So the Internet is something relatively recent, younger than me, and I witnessed its birth.

And it is still a marvel, in the strict sense of the term. The marvel of successful communication. Concretely, it is a somewhat Deleuzian world, a support-surface aesthetics against the backdrop of a brain machine: with its network, its rhizome—center everywhere and circumference nowhere—its multiplicities, subsidiaries, direct power of the multitude, simplicity of connection, self-organization,

BOX A

What I Always Wanted to Know but Was Afraid to Ask: A Brief Immediate History of the Internet and the Web

The Internet, which is an abbreviation of "Interconnected Networks," is the worldwide network connecting all networks, which all the computers in the world can connect to. Its ancestor is the Arpanet, created in 1969 by the US Department of Defense. The starting point was wholly pragmatic: How can a single terminal communicate with several computing centers? The result, however, is that communication is no longer reliant on a single, strategically vulnerable center; with a network there are multiple heterogeneous layers, each with its own communications protocol, language, and channel (telephone line, fiber optic cable, or satellite), and multiple centers (50 percent of the world's Internet traffic still passes through the state of Virginia). The Internet enables the whole world to be interconnected, and France has been connected to it since 1988.[1]

Its other is the intranet (or rather intranets), networks that are not worldwide, but each one confined, *intra*, to a business or a university, for example. An intranet can, of course, be connected to the Internet, and one can also erect barriers inside the Internet. The new Wall of China that the government is building at the heart of the Internet in China, censoring opposition websites or information and images it disapproves of, reduces the Chinese Internet to a vast, politically correct intranet. Google, after Yahoo!, has just given in to censorship as a condition of the market.[2] Like any successful censorship (following the age-old principle according to which supreme art is a matter of hiding its artfulness), it covers its tracks so that the user is not aware there is any censorship. From the moment it began operating in China, Google decided, as if obeying the command of a Chinese "Patriot Act," that prohibited addresses would not even generate an error message.

The Internet is based on the TCP/IP (Transmission Control Protocol/Internet Protocol), a worldwide system of addresses of communication protocols. These addresses are now assigned and managed by ICANN (Internet Corporation for Assigned Names and Numbers), a nonprofit organization with a hybrid status, half-private and half-public, and neither truly international nor truly American. Founded in 1998 following international pressure, ICANN took over the functions of the IANA (International Assigned Numbers Authority), which was accountable only to its effective creator, the American government, and it signed a protocol agreement with the US Department of Commerce that is still in force, even though it was initially intended to be for a period of five years, or until 2003. This organization is responsible in particular for domain names (DNS, or Domain Name System), like .org, .com, .net, but also .fr, and more recently .eu,[3] and so on, and of course invents new ones, following a strict ratio (seven in the year 2000, including .biz, .info, and .museum). Its power was felt recently when it refused to assign a domain name to "adult only" sites and create a "red light district" on the Web. It could (could it?) decide to wipe out a whole section of the Internet, to virtually "unrealize" a country. In any event, decisions are made in and around Washington, where Google also has an office. It is worth noting, moreover, that a search engine such as Google makes the work of ICANN less meaningful, since it allows one to find an address without going through a domain name.

Each computer in its turn is identified by an IP address, which is its identity card. This is how one can trace a search back to a computer, and a computer back to its buyer, even an email back to its user, author, or addressee. Whence the perfectly justifiable fear that a *Big Brother* could know "everything" if it wanted to, that is, provided it sees an interest, and gives itself the means to do so.

The Internet makes services such as the *network time protocol*, email, file sharing and transfer, phone networks, and the *World Wide Web*, the global spider web, accessible to the public. The WWW (are we allowed to hear this as World Wild Web, suggesting a certain wildness in its wideness?) is not itself synonymous with the Internet. The original idea, which was conceived in 1989 by Tim Berners-Lee, who at the time was an IT engineer at the European Organization for Nuclear Research (CERN) in Geneva, was to link together all of the servers in the whole world, by creating a server for these servers, a kind of metaserver, which was indeed organized into a worldwide network in 1992. It has three main functions: to serve as a multimedia platform, to integrate preexisting services, and, most important, to navigate using hypertext. Access to the network's resources effectively happens through documents formatted in HTML (Hypertext Markup Language). What is significant about HTML code is that it enables hypertext links, or "pointers" which you simply need to click in order to connect to other servers, or to access specific information. These pointers, linked for example to keywords, contain three pieces of information: the type of protocol to use, the name of the server, and the name of the file in that server. This is how a Web address is interpreted, for example: http (hypertext transfer protocol) [= the protocol]; www (World Wide Web) [= the server]; .google [= the file within that server]. Navigation software then provides a number of different entry portals (or browsers, such as Netscape or Internet Explorer), which allow one to consult documents.

The network as a whole is made up materially of analog or digital telephone lines, of fiber optic cables a micron in diameter, of larger cables, and of satellites. Yes, the immaterial network is material, concrete, made of things, which lie on the seabed or cross the sky. Units of bits circulate along these materials, as they do via satellite. The term "bit" is a contraction of "binary digit," but by chance it also in natural language means "fragment, small amount, piece."[4] It is the unit of measure in information technology, and refers to the basic quantity of information: 0 or 1 in digital code ("open" or "closed" in electronics, "false" or "true" in logic). All information is coded in bits, and philosophers are in rhapsodies at the idea that Leibniz, the inventor of infinitesimal calculus, could have simultaneously thought of the universal characteristic (an attempt to write algebraically the essence of each individual or particular), the principle of indiscernibles (no particular differs from another *solo numero*, and if two particulars have the same formula, they become one), and the principle of reason (there has to be a reason why something is the way it is rather than any other way, in order for there to be something rather than nothing), and that Boole proved him right with his binary code of 0 and 1.

None of this can really be understood if we ignore the fact that it is historically American, that the United States was its inventor and architect, and it is one of the effects of the network that it has been shared. One can build using locks and dams, as many providers in fact have. As Huitema says, "For a network provider to be able to offer an Internet service, it really only has to be connected, or directed through the intermediary of a partner, at the main point of interconnection, which is in the United States, in a suburb of Washington."[5] It truly is the image of a self-regulating market, one compelled by a principle of virtue, in which "it is in everyone's interest to cooperate, and to maintain global connectivity." Huitema is merciless on this score: "Just a few years ago [he is writing in 1995] the Internet was perceived as being entirely under American control. Even though the American army no longer played any part in their adoption, in France the standards of the Internet were called

'DoD standards.' There is of course no longer any need nowadays to fear control by the American government" (84). "The majority of members of the IAB (Internet Architecture Board) and of the IESG (Internet Engineering Steering Group, which pilots the IETF, Internet Engineering Task Force, a group of volunteers responsible for developing Internet standards) are of course American, but this is simply a reflection of how deeply involved American industry is." As always, Athenian democracy comes to the rescue: "The procedures [for election to the IAB] are in fact copied from Athenian democracy. Every year they draw lots from a list of volunteers for a 'nominating committee'" (82). "But even if it had once been true that the rules could only be fixed by the Americans, it would have been better to adopt them than to become tangled up in a strategy that is doomed to failure." (85) "Of course, you have to speak English, but that is also the case for every standardisation group" (85).

Keep moving, there is nothing to see here, unless we take things right back to the start, with Louis Pouzin, "the man who did not invent the Internet,"[6] a promoter in the 1970s of the French network Cyclades, a rival to Arpanet. He is now working at the NLIC (Native Language Internet Consortium) and at Netpia (Native Language Internet Address), promoting multilingualism, including in the alphabet of web addresses: "To challenge monolingualism is to challenge American hegemony . . . there is no technical necessity for it to be this way [making the system of DNS addresses work with unaccented Latin characters]: the only 'necessity' is to preserve the current system as it is because it is run in the United States."

NOTES

1. See the short, already dated book by Christian Huitema, *Et Dieu créa l'Internet . . .* (Paris: Eyrolles, 1995), which tells the story of the

Internet through his own experience at the CNET (Centre National d'Études sur les Télécommunications), at the INRIA (Institut National de Recherche en Informatique et Automatique), and as president of the IAB (Internet Activities Board, which was renamed the Internet Architecture Board in 1993).

2. See *Libération* (February 15, 2006) and Chapter 4 of this book on the relationship between Google and states. More recently, when I was last in China in 2015, every morning began with a student coming to my hotel room to take down the censorship barriers.

3. On the perfectly legal opaqueness of the attribution of the domain name .eu, for example, see the article from April 2006 in *Le Monde*. The procedure was entrusted to Eurid, a nonprofit organization based in Brussels, and selected by the EU. As we read on the Eudomaindesaster website, however, "200,000 domain names have been monopolized by about fifteen companies (the city of Dublin, for example, had its domain names stolen), with a net worth of 100 million euros." And Cyprus allegedly has as many domain names ending in .eu as France, that is, around 75,000.

4. To pursue this homophony with Wikipedia, "byte" in English nowadays means "octet" (a unit of eight bits, the smallest possible unit), and when pronounced in French, it is at the very least a source of confusion, not to mention obviously the term bit itself, which in French "presents a certain homonymous ambiguity" (one could avoid this indecency in French, according to Wikipedia, by talking about *chib*, an abbreviation of *chiffre binaire* [binary number]). [*Bite* or *bitte* is rather coarse slang for penis. The irony here is that *chib* is more or less equivalent slang in French to *bite*. —Trans.]

5. Huitema, *Et Dieu créa l'Internet*, 73. Subsequent page references are given in the text.

6. This is the title of an article from *Le Monde* of August 5, 2006, from which the final quotation is taken.

and so on. A world made by everyone, immanently, and not by one, in which Deleuze meets Lautréamont ("Poetry must be made by all. Not one.") and Rimbaud is read by Char ("its incendiary date is rapidity").[6] In the face of such a "resolutely modern" world, the only battles would ever be rearguard ones. Unless . . . unless, of course, certain "new" values turn out to be even more stereotyped and outmoded that the old ones, because they are taken firmly in hand by the most outdated of the new worlds: *Don't be evil . . .*

A PHILOLOGIST ON THE WEB

Subjectively, at any rate, this upheaval is all the more immense given how imperceptible it has been and how much it has already become integrated into our lives. The Internet is fatal to philological methodology ("philo-logy" means a love of language, of languages, of spoken and written words), which is the very methodology that has been used to construct "our culture": respecting the word, and taking pleasure in works of literature or art. We are, Nietzsche said, like a centaur that limps along as it puts one leg in front of the other. We do indeed have total respect for texts: We critique sources, we create editions of texts, we obsessively verify the accuracy of the written word; but then we also produce works that are singular in style and take pleasure and total enjoyment in language.[7] At any rate, you cannot have the one without the other.

Well, panic stations on the Web! When it comes to the obsession with and rigor of literal sources that are a condition of the integrity of citationality, nothing is reliable. Pleasure in the singular, whether of style or of a work, is precisely what cannot be taken into account, essentially-right-now (if I might venture this syntagm).

Nothing is reliable in at least two senses of the term.

Flow and the haystack

On this Web, which we "crawl" or "surf" across, sources are in a state of constant flux, and we are in the Heraclitean world of fluctuating, even flowing, identities, in the sense in which Plato said Heracliteans were all suffering from colds and were incapable of grasping any idea, or essence, or stable identity. The most we can do is to indicate a source by the name of a website (which will disappear) and by a kind of timestamp that refers to an inventory in a given place, or rather in a given time, which has by definition vanished. Except that the pages have a temporary afterlife by being stored as a "cached" bookmark by Google, which shows the inventories immediately before this one, the immediate history of the webpage consulted and its updates (unless, of course, the site has disappeared, and its links along with it). They have an eternal, quasi-Mormon afterlife too, within the Internet Archive, which is open to all.[8]

The absence of criteria: The example of Wikipedia

There is also no guarantee of reliability on the Web, in the sense of the truth of the information found there. The fact that everything is "information," and thus on the same level, does not help us to discriminate. The paradigm for this is Wikipedia, "the free encyclopedia that anyone can edit." Created in 2001 by Jimmy Wales, it contains, as I write, more than 3 million articles in 212 languages (923,102 articles exist in English, as opposed to 224,925 for Wikipedia France),[9] all caught up in the flow—*wiki wiki* means "quick" in Hawaiian. It is an attempt to "create and distribute freely a free encyclopedia, of the best possible quality, to everyone on the planet in his or her own language."[10] Poetry will be made by all, and so the encyclopedia will be created by everyone, but, as Heidegger used to complain of conferences, why would understanding necessarily emerge from an accumulation of misunderstandings?

It may well be that there is no "standard," but it works, as the site explains, as long as we are only dealing with "uncontroversial topics," such as the critique of Wikipedia within Wikipedia, which is an excellent self-critique: anti-elitism as a kind of weakness, systematic bias of content and perspective, the difficulty of monitoring facts, the use of dubious sources, vandalism, and so on. Jimmy

BOX B

Alexandria, Alex(andr)a, or Capitalism
and Schizophrenia

Internet Archive, a private nonprofit program, was founded by Brewster Kahle in 1996. It retains daily copies of the World Wide Web and constitutes a digital library of the Web, as well as of all its other artifacts (music, films, and so on). It is a "way-back machine," a machine that goes back in time; to describe it using the term "total recall" is not an exaggeration. According to its site, the program has archived 40 million Web pages in order to constitute a "New Library of Alexandria, Egypt," but one that has the foresight to preserve several copies (yes, you can write not only to San Francisco, but also to Bibliotheca Alexandrina, P.O. Box 138, El Shatby, Alexandria 21526, Egypt). An even wider dissemination is planned with two other centers in Asia and in Europe. The objective is clear—"To preserve the heritage of humanity and to ensure access to this heritage"—and if, outside of this movement, you do not want someone crawling through your website ("someone" here meaning a robot), you can declare this and exempt yourself ("robot exclusion"). Otherwise, you will be a needle that can always be found in the worldwide haystack.

Along with Bruce Gilliat, Brewster Kahle also founded in 1996 a profit-making company, with the same know-how and the same type of program. "Alexa" is a commercial offshoot that Amazon.com bought for $250 million in 1999. So this is how it always seems to be: a philanthropic, humanitarian objective, and an objective to be intensely profitable, both in the same hand, or rather left hand and right hand. One for God's sake, and one for the sake of the stock exchange, an updated Protestant ethic, or capitalism and schizophrenia, if you like. As we will see, this is more or less the same structure as Google, which even though it is characterized by its public rejection of advertising (including of the company itself, whose success is due to word of mouth), makes 99 percent of its income from advertising. Except that with Google there are not two companies with two different functions, but two places on the same page: the organic center, and the sponsored margins (see Chapter 4). Is the infrastructure of the American *mētis*[1] also our infrastructure?

Having said that, any page selected at random from the Internet Archive could hardly be called sexy, and it is easy to see why it can be compared to a haystack. Today, January 14, 2006, this is the opening paragraph of the daily inventory:

> The most recent additions to the Internet Archive collections.
>
> The RSS feed is generated dynamically tracey@archive.org Sat. 14 Jan 2006 04:41 PST A special "Good Morning Davina McCall" Jingle. This item belongs to: audio/ourmedia. This item has files of the following types: mpeg Sat. 14 Jan 2006 04:30:23 PST audio/ourmedia Test Podcast . . . enjoy. This item belongs to: Sound/ourmedia. This item has files of the following types: audio (including music), 64Kbps MP3, 128Kbps M3U, 64Kbps M3U, 128Kbps MP3, Ogg Vorbis, 64Kbps MP3 ZIP Sat. 14 Jan 2006 04:30:18 PST http:// creativecommons.org/licenses/by-sa/2.5/Sound/ourmedia. The special "Good Morning Boutros Boutros Ghali" Jingle. This item belongs to audio/ourmedia. This item has files of the following types: mpeg Sat. 14 Jan 2006 04:30:03 PST audio/ourmedia A special "Good morning Peter Crouch" Jingle. This item belongs to: audio/ourmedia. This item has files of the following types: mpeg Sat 14. Jan 2006 04:30:01 PT audio/ourmedia A special "Good Morning James Beaty" Jingle. This item belongs to: audio/ourmedia. This item has files of the following types: mpeg Sat. 14 Jan 2006 04:30:00 PST audio/ourmedia A special "Good Morning David O'Leary" Jingle. This item belongs to: audio/ourmedia. This

item has files of the following types: mpeg Sat. 14 Jan 2006 04:29:50 PST audio/ourmedia The new and improved One Road Travel Jingle. This item belongs to: audio/ourmedia. This item has files of the following types: mpeg Sat. Ja 14 Jan 2006 04:28:05 PST audio/ourmedia Chris and the team discuss "Deal or No Deal" This item belong to audio/ourmedia. This item has files of the following types: mpeg Sat 14. Jan 2006 04:27:04 PST audio/ourmedia A song sang by Kylie Minogue. This item belongs to audio/ourmedia. This item has files of the following types: mpeg Sat 14. Jan 2006 04:26:53 PST audio/ourmedia Creative Root Radio Test Podcast. This item belongs to: Sound/ourmedia. This item has files of the following types: audio (including music), 64Kbps MP3, 128Kbps M3U, 64Kbps M3U, 128Kbps MP3, Ogg Vorbis, 64Kbps MP3 ZIP Sat. 14 Jan 2006 04:25:25 PST http://creativecommons.org/licences/by-sa/2.5/Sound/ ourmedia Juste la video de madame Metzger qui passe devant nous. . . .

We should add that Brewster Kahle recently initiated the Open Content Alliance (OCA), which we will come back to in relation to Google Book Search and other digital libraries. It was founded in order to scan 170,000 works in all languages, and by December 2005 it was up to twelve.[2] Brewster Kahle, along with Tim Berners-Lee, is without a doubt a key figure and entrepreneur for what is to follow.

NOTES

1. *Mētis* is the Greek term that characterizes the cunning of Ulysses and the Promethean intelligence of the Sophists.

2. These figures are taken from an article by Andreas von Bubnoff, "The Real Death of Print," *Nature* 438 (December 2005). On digital libraries, see Chapter 5. [As of 2016, there were more than 3 million freely available e-books to borrow. —Trans.]

Wales does, however, envisage a "standardized," stabilized version, one that is "revised in such a way that we can trust it,"[11] that would coexist on the site alongside the "live" version, that itself could require the Internet user to register online in order to publish.

By its own admission, Wikipedia works well as long as everyone agrees—*doxa* as opposed to *agōn*, or received opinion as opposed to confrontation and the process of questioning. No controversial topics, nothing but transparency, and everyone will be in agreement, like Bouvard and Pécuchet.[12] From a soft, weak *doxa* to a soft, weak style. Whatever item you open is useful if you know nothing about it and deplorable when you know a little about it (search for "Plato," for example). Here we touch upon one of the key problems, which Google tackles head-on with the PageRank algorithm: Does quantity produce quality? Is the "each and every one," the all made up of one plus one, a guarantee of universality, and a guarantee of democracy? What does it mean to give to those who don't know, what those who do know do not want to have for themselves? Surely one of the main challenges for every form of teaching and every form of pedagogy today is learning how to use the Internet, learning to "critique," to problematize, and to construct just as much as to search, find, and cut and paste.[13] This is all very uncontroversial, good for all men of goodwill, but it is not so easy to extricate oneself from the confusion between information and culture.

As for the pleasure of the philologist, the singularity of style and of the work, there is little point in even thinking about it any more. It will clearly not emerge suddenly from Wikipedia, nor from the form of the information given, which will always require a sociological rather than literary analysis. This is perhaps what blogs pick up on, each blogger staking their claim to be an author, a commentator on themselves and their world, opening the intimacy of their lives to discussion, with the attendant risk of an infinite inflation of self-authorized authors without a work, as well as the utter discouragement of the finite reader, or the reader who is finished off, in all senses of the term. What is freighted across the Internet is a complex of information-opinions free from the traditional demands of truth and evidence, without satisfying the demands of taste either. It is true that taste is formed and is in the process of changing, but the content of the Internet and the form this content is given are perfectly adapted to one another by Google.

So what is it about Google that is so singular?

2

GOOGLE INC.: FROM SEARCH TO GLOBAL CAPITAL

THE NAME THAT BECAME A VERB

A good way into Google, into the culture of Google, is through its name. "Yahoo!" is taken from western slang. AltaVista and eBay are a kind of opening out of information technology onto the California horizon. What does "Google" mean to us?

"I google," "google me," "I feel googled": The fact that the name has become a verb is the surest sign of its global success. I will begin, then, with this name, which, somewhere between a private joke and a cartoon onomatopoeia, flirts with meaning and with immediacy, all the more marketable because its dangerous aggression is softened by a kind of schoolboy humor, making it appear quite inoffensive. Google, I would even stretch it out to Goooooogle, with as many Os (the letter) and as many 0s (the number) as you wish.

One of the symptoms of success is that the name sometimes becomes eponymous: Look at "*vespasienne*" (the French term for public urinal), or "Macintosh" (a Scot, a waterproof coat, and above all a variety of apple, closer to a Red Delicious than a Reinette, bought by and for Steve Jobs's Mac, the apple being of course Newton's apple, without which he would not have discovered gravity, and so on—how harmless and how full of promise for a computer). Or sometimes the brand name becomes a generic name, as with the French "*frigidaire*" (fridge). In this case, the Name has become a Verb, and the expression "to google" has become synonymous with "to search for on the Internet" (as in the famous old song, "*Je cherche après Titine*," I am searching for Titine . . .). Not only "I google," actively, but I google something, transitively and objectively, and I am googled, passively, or indeed, I google myself, reflexively, so as to find out what people can see of me, updated from one day to the next.

The account of how it began, which has all the makings of a myth (too full of meaning, and different versions that are equally meaningful), is narrated in detail by Vise.[1] Toward the end of 1997, two young students, Lawrence Page and Sergey Brin, wanted to find a new name for the search engine they concocted as part of their doctoral thesis. They originally called it "BackRub," because it was the first to take into account backlinks, rather than just the links that led out from it. The word they chose was "Googol," 1 plus 1,000 zeros, a word invented by the young Melton Sirotta, the nine-year-old nephew of the American mathematician Edward Kasner, who popularized it in his book, coauthored with James Newman, *Mathematics and the Imagination*. A fortunate misspelling on the computer supposedly produced Google, fortunate because Googol was already taken. Unless it was not a mistake, but a choice: "We chose our system name, Google, because it is a common spelling of googol, or 10^{100} and fits well with our goal of building very large-scale search engines," Brin and Page said when they presented their invention for the first time at Stanford.[2] Or unless it was actually "a play on the word googol."[3] As with the word "quark,"[4] it is something of a free-floating signifier, smart in all senses of the term, witty and affectedly stylish, the preserve of an elite brought up on the humor of Lewis Carroll and portmanteau words, with Joyce in the background, a private joke elevated to the level of the universal.

And with the quintessentially British game of cricket on the horizon: The slang expression "to throw a googly" means something like "to ask a deceptive question," because in cricket, a "googly" is a ball whose flight is difficult to anticipate, and very difficult to play, and the *Chambers Twentieth Century Dictionary* (1972) derives the verb "to google" from it. It is, however, the meaning "to look" which one hears first of all: The verb "to ogle" means "to gape, to gawk," and "googly" is used of someone who casts a tender look.[5]

With a gurgle, "we giggle at the Google-doodles," the logo that Google joyfully decorates for holidays and other important occasions. They never miss Saint Patrick, or the Chinese New Year, or Mothers' Day, and celebrate the birthdays of Michelangelo, Picasso, Van Gogh, Conan Doyle, and Martin Luther King, more or less stylishly. Google also militates against AIDS, with the Os as two perfectly round but slightly shriveled condoms, and the message to "do it with."[6]

The logo by itself says what it has to say, simple, colorful, drawn for big kids, American and otherwise, from seven to seventy-seven years old. It is Tintin in the land of Rimbaud's vowels, *o* red, *o* yellow, *e* red, *g* blue, and *l* green. Isolated on the page: We will return to this idea, because this page that is visited so frequently contains no advertising whatsoever, which is precisely its most extreme act of self-publicity, the art of hiding its artfulness, *ars celare artem*, so well known in rhetoric.

In short, this playfulness of the signifier and its good-luck number is part of the culture of Google. It was floated on the stock exchange on Friday 13. In its IPO, Google wanted to raise "*e*" (= $2,718,261,828), and in its offer in August 2005, it sold 14,159,265 shares (all the decimals of "pi").[7]

WHAT INVENTION EXACTLY? THE ANATOMY OF A BIG TOOL

Sergey Brin and Larry Page met in 1995 at Stanford, where they were enrolled in the Computer Science and Technology doctoral

BOX C

Google and James Joyce: Looking Tenderly

Google: the name has been read as a concatenation of the words "Go ogle," even if it is generally agreed that this is a coincidence. The word "google" appears in *Finnegans Wake* and is not really translated in the recent French translation by Philippe Lavergne, which is not something we can hold against him.[1]

> [I:8 231:12] His mouthfull of ecstasy (for Shing-Yung-Thing in Shina from Yoruyume across the Timor Sea), herepong (maladventure!) shot pinging up through the errorooth of his wisdom (who thought him a Fonar all, feastking of shellies by googling Lovvey, regally freytherem, eagelly plumed . . .

> *Ses bouffées d'extase (auparavant chinois de la jeunesse de l'autre côté de la Mer Sargastique du Temps), ses coups de harponts (malaventre!) jetés entre les errorhizomes de sa sagesse (qui l'a jamais pris pour Fonar le barde, Percy Feastyking Shelley, Lovelace, le frère royal, plume d'aigle . . .* (358–359).

Or, in Jean Dixsaut's translation, which is more attentive to Google:[2]

> *Sa bouchée d'extase (pour Célesteville chez les Célestes en venant de Yoyohama par la mer du Tempspête) là-dessus (malheure!) remonta pong-ping entre les dents de sa sagesse (quilupris pour un bardophone se roipaissant de shelleys en zyeutant Lovelacet . . .*

And to complete the picture, these are the search results for "googl*," followed in each case by Lavergne's translation:

> [2:8 265.4] *Googlaa pluplu.*

> *Glouglou pluplu* (411).

[3:14 584.9] He'll win your toss, flog your old tom's bowling and I darr ye, barrackybuller, to break his duck! He's posh. I lob him. We're parring all Oogster till the empsyseas run googlie. Declare to ashes and teste his metch! Three for two will do for me and he for thee and she for you.

Il gagnera ta toison, fouettera la case de l'oncle Tom et si j'ose dire, ton baraquement écurieux, pour casser trois pattes à un canard! Son havre. Je l'aime. Toutes voiles dehors jusqu'à ce que l'empyre des mers devienne coupé à droite du batteur. Affirmer sur les cendres et faire épreuve du feu! Trois pour deux pour moi et lui pour toi et elle pour toi (861).

[4:15 620.22] And when them two has had a good few there isn't much more dirty clothes to publish. From the Laundersdale Missions. One chap googling the holyboy's thingabib and this lad wetting his widdle.

Et quand ils ont leur crise tous les deux, il n'y a plus beaucoup de linge sale à étaler. Ils reviennent de la blanchisserie des quatre chemins. Y'a l'aîné qui louche sur le bout du doigt du petit Jésus et le petit qui mouille ses langes (911).

There are in these quotations different layers of language (as on the Internet), with cricket references (in quotation 3, bowling, slips, duck, lob, bye, googlie, perhaps even ashes), and erotic or pornographic allusions (the holyboy's thing-abib?). This is all caught up in the dance of the signifier, to the sound of noodle, and poodle. One can also hear "gaggle" (as in a gaggle of geese, or of gabbling women), "gargle," and "gur-gle" ("gurgle" = "make a bubbling sound as of liquid escaping intermittently from a bottle or of water flowing among stones," and "utter broken guttural cries").

But it suggests above all, of course, looking and eyes, and

it is clear that in quotations 1 and 4 the verb that we hear is indeed "ogle." "Ogle" means "stare at," "stare at lecherously ("lecherously" = "having or showing excessive or offensive sexual desire"), impertinently, flirtatiously, or amorously," and as a noun, "a lecherous look," "an impertinent, flirtatious, or amorous stare."

Finally, the *Oxford English Dictionary* gives two definitions for "googly," which first appeared at the beginning of the twentieth century:

1. (Noun) Cricket: A ball which breaks from the off, though bowled with apparent leg-break action. Figurative: A deceptive question.
2. (Adjective). Of eyes: large, round and staring. Of a person, disposed to love-making.

One also finds "goo-goo," as an adjective: (of the eyes or glances) amorous. An amorous glance, colloquial, "with goo-goo eyes."

Related to "goggle," verb and adjective, said of a person and of their eyes: protuberant, prominent, full, and rolling, particularly as a result of being puzzled or surprised, or when one rolls one's eyes, and looks with wide eyes. In the plural, "goggles" refers to glasses that protect eyes from the sun or from dust (e.g., a motorcyclist's goggles), "goggle-eyed" (e.g., "goggle-box," slang for a television set).

A journalist from the *San Jose Mercury-News* was clearly aware of this eponymy when he wrote "If Google ogles your e-mail, could Ashcroft [the US Attorney General] be far behind?" (quoted in a *Playboy* interview in September 2004). Google ogles over your shoulder whenever you write an email, adding to the apple pie recipe your mom sends you all of the apple pie recipes from the cookbooks that have paid for this, to try to get you to buy them. Google, through a vicarious robot, sees everything, and looks at you with goo-goo eyes, only offering you what interests you—this is its style of flirting, with every one of you, while giving you the impression of being unique. We will come back to this with the PageRank algorithm and "bigbrotherization."

NOTES

1. *Finnegans Wake*, translated from the English, presented and adapted [*sic*] by Philippe Lavergne (Paris: Gallimard, 1997; reissue, Folio, 2001). The text of *Finnegans Wake* is accessible on the Internet at http://www.trentu.ca/jjoyce. The pagination retains that of the 1939 Faber edition. See also the concordance: Finnegans Wake Concordex, mv.lycaeum/org/Finnegan/. [Rather than elide the French in the present translation, it seemed all the more pertinent to retain it, not only for Cassin's comments, but to foreground the way in which "google" itself in Joyce's text becomes something of an "Untranslatable" in its own right. —Trans.]

2. I am indebted to Jean Dixsaut for this entire note.

program. They had much in common, both young, fit, good-looking guys with wide smiles and an appetite for discussion.[8] They were both born in 1973, in families of Jewish origin, although not religious. Sergey Brin was born in Moscow, where his father, Michael, a mathematician, worked as an economist for Gosplan, and his mother, also a mathematician, as a civil engineer. The Brins emigrated in 1979, and his father taught mathematics at the University of Maryland, while NASA recruited his mother.[9] Larry Page was born in Michigan. His father Carl was one of the first to obtain a degree in computer technology, which he taught at the University of Michigan, and which his two sons, Carl Jr. and Larry, also studied, while his wife was a data consultant. Brin and Page were educated in Montessori schools; they both had parents who were professors, and scientifically minded mothers (then stepmother for Larry), and this made them second-generation information technologists, as if it were second nature to them, and they were naturally competent.

I feel like telling their story in English, because it is such an American dream: two *clever young fellows* who grew up in the Silicon Valley *boom*, then *crash*, and who felt *empowered* to change the world. It was because they were good students, full of respect for the academic world and the University model, that they would go on to become great inventors and superrich entrepreneurs.

Brin and Page noticed, like everyone else, that search engines were astonishingly bad: They produced a mass of unusable results because they were repetitive and irrelevant and poorly prioritized relative to the question asked. How can I get access to what "I" am searching for? In short, how does one build a good search engine? As Brin and Page explain, in the interview they gave to *Playboy* in 2004, search as such was of no interest to anyone because it did not directly generate income. In 1997–98, the way was clear at any rate for an altruistic invention that no one could reasonably suspect would become so profitable.

What is a search engine? Elementary, my dear Watson. A search engine on one level gives answers to queries, and the *relevance* of the answers determines its quality. It "*crawls*" data (or *browses* it), on all fours, creeping around, swimming, grazing, it goes around the web like a *spider*, or like a *worm* (the robot that is the search engine is a protean swarm of metaphors), and then it indexes them. On another level, it analyzes queries, essentially using keywords. Finally, it provides relevant answers and classifies them thanks to a *runtime system*, or *query processor*, a type of *software* that makes the connections between the queries and the data index.

For a search engine to be good, that is, for it to provide relevant answers in an appropriate order, one has to (and it is sufficient to) optimize each stage. But the shift in scale, with the exponential growth of the Web and the number of searches, produced a real step change. It was this shift in scale that Brin and Page, our two

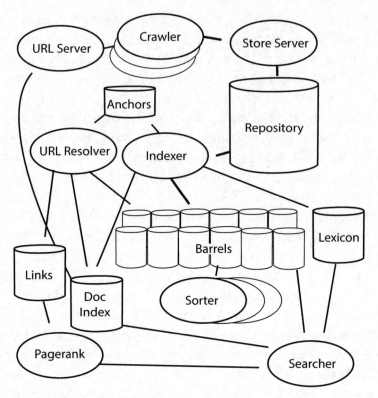

Google architecture overview

young students who never took the time to complete their PhDs, tried to come to terms with, in the first, clear and historically moving explanation of Google in embryonic form that they presented on the steps of the Computer Science department at Stanford in 1998. The title was quite Dadaist: "The Anatomy of a Large-Scale Hypertextual Web Search Engine."[10]

This is the anatomical schema: Google Stripped Bare By Its Inventors, Even. And what did they find, at least in part, but the timeless anatomy of *logos*: scanning, selecting, gathering, storing, so as to make, from one indexed barrel to another, something like a new art of memory.[11]

So Google would have to:

1. Quantitatively, store as much data as possible by crawling as many sites as possible. As soon as he came to Stanford, "with a healthy nonchalance with regard to the impossible," Page already wanted to "download the entirety of the Web onto his computer."[12] When Brin and Page presented their "Anatomy," their system used four crawlers that, combined, could scan a hundred pages per second. Today Google can scan the entirety of the visible Web[13] (11.5 billion pages) in about a month.

The "anatomical" schema shows us the huge barrels that contain, in compressed form, the crawled pages. It is easy to see the importance of the hardware and, very concretely, of the number of computers used. This is one of the distinctive strengths of Google, due to the way itself that the company was set up, accumulating ordinary computers in rooms, student offices, garages. It also explains why this computer infrastructure is so cheap and robust, and why it works like an army of foot soldiers, marching in parallel formation—the more of them there are, the better it is, since if one breaks, the others take over, and this "distributed computing" is now the rule. By all accounts, there are today more than 100,000 computers linked together in this way—amounting to who knows how many servers (10,000? 250,000? estimates vary wildly)—and using a simplified version of Linux, with a proportion of these constantly on the move, in trucks, or as cargo, to be used as reinforcements when needed.

2. Qualitatively, index data in the best possible way. In order to index this data, it has to be analyzed and tagged, that is to say labeled, so it can be sorted and located. At the core of the analysis are "keywords." We are asked to choose a certain number ourselves whenever we write an article, or even when we deposit a thesis at the Sorbonne, but Googlebot, the robot that does this crawling for Google, also indexes every word on the whole page from a basic vocabulary (14 million in 1998, and 8 billion in some thirty-five languages today).[14] It takes into account, in ever more sophisticated ways, the parameters of the word's appearance (its frequency, but

also its place in the document—such as an address, a title, a foot-note—and even the font, the size, or whether it is lower or upper case). Each document is thus transformed into a set of occurrences or "hits."[15] Indexation is then usable in two senses: The direct index takes us from documents to words, but the sorting mechanism sub-sequently generates an inverse index, which takes us from words to documents, in order to produce answers.

The indices that refer us to the data are in turn organized by means of metadata. This data about the data can be internal to the data itself (it indicates the language used, the type of vocabulary, the group it belongs to when the detection criteria can be estab-lished, and before they are turned away—such as spam or pornog-raphy, for example—information about the address—email, ZIP codes, for example—and the type or format—text, HTML, images, and so on), and can be generated automatically by machines (the "logfile" or "output" of a database). It can also be external to the data, and made up of information that one can infer from the docu-ment, but that is not contained within it, for example the source type, its "quality," the update frequency, the number of visitors it has, and the number of references made to it. So next to the key-words one finds "cue words" or "tags," quasi-concepts which are used to classify and organize: for example, in "Lincoln biography," "Lincoln" is a key word, which one has to find as a content, but the tag "biography" indicates the literary genre. Google's great original-ity is that it indexes not only the links that lead out from a page but also the links that lead back to it. Its indexing system thus gener-ates a database of links that are pairs of documents that have been identified, with "anchor texts" from which these links lead out. It is from this database, which is weighted, that PageRank is calculated.

3. Analyze queries using the best possible method. This analysis works in two ways. First, by a direct analysis of the query using keywords, and here Google prompts you to query better. Not only does it make suggestions, or correct spellings, for example ("try with the following spelling"), and disambiguate keywords, suggest-

ing shortcuts ("I'm feeling lucky"), but it invites you to participate in something like an art or a sport of the query, by allowing you to use a quasi-syntax, with items in order, connecters ("everything except"), less common terms, or playing around with the metadata.[16] Second, you can improve the analysis by profiling. A "personalized search" retains the memory of the previous queries, so the traces of the user's visits and choices (memorized by the cookies left on his or her computer, and the "clickstream")[17] are so many clues to the kind of problem he or she is asking about, as well as to the kind of answer deemed satisfactory.

4. Give the best possible answers to queries, by providing a list of relevant URL addresses, with a more or less explicit description of their content. One has to know first of all how to eliminate redundant information, those interminable lists of the same site which reappear in the ranking, not to mention the spam, including pornographic spam, that foregrounds repeated keywords that have nothing to do with their actual content.

The answer also has to be understood, that is, in the language of the person asking the question. Google now offers an interface in 104 languages or dialects, with a personalized version of the search engine for 138 countries. Google South Africa also has an interface in Afrikaans, in Xhosa, in Zulu, and in Sesotho, and it can, in a number of cases, limit the search to the local Web (this is just as possible for the island of Malta or for Kyrgyzstan as it is for England or Taiwan). But the relevance of the answers depends most crucially on the way they are ranked. In the answer to a multiple query, every search engine ranks more or less well, according to the match with the words of the query, by weighting the proximity of all of the words, and then of a few words. Besides this kind of "IR score," Google uses a ranking algorithm called PageRank that determines relevance depending on the links, and weights the one relative to the other to determine the rank. This is what accounts for the quality of its answers. It is worth carrying out an experiment on the difference between Yahoo! and Google, as John Battelle does, for

example, when he types in the word "Usher": With Google, one gets
Poe as early as page 2, while with Yahoo!, all one gets is the singer
(his website also appears in Google's "I'm feeling lucky"), unless
one types Usher Poe. So you will never know through Yahoo!, un-
less you already knew it, that Edgar Allan Poe wrote "The Fall of the
House of Usher." And it is also via Google that a certain Monsieur
Cambe not long ago identified the Hugo quotation in Flaubert's
"Pyrenees-Corsica."[18]

In short, PageRank, which we will analyze in detail, is one of the
keys to Google's secret.

"CASH-POOR AND IDEA-RICH": A CAPITALIST SAGA

Brin and Page tried to license their discovery to the major players
in Silicon Valley, but to no avail, since search was not a priori profitable. Indeed, this was what made the "Google Guys" likeable for
so long.

Let us remind ourselves of the different stages of what is quite
a transparent saga, and which is moreover available from Google
(these are the *milestones* of their *corporate information*). It is a
tale of two students living on a shoestring, of do-it-yourself buddies
in dorm rooms with wires all over the place, of sleeping in labs,
of things found at the backs of drawers, of a girlfriend's garage,
and of the astonished word of mouth of the first users. Google is
originally hosted on Stanford University's website, google.stanford
.edu, and then the domain name google.com is registered on September 7, 1997.

In 1998, Andy Bechtolsheim, the founder of Sun, makes the initial investment of $100,000 to buy the computers, even before the
creation of the company Google Inc., the name to which the check
is already made out. Ten thousand queries a day arrive while the
search engine is still in its experimental beta version. Stories in the
world's press (*USA Today* and *Le Monde*; *PC Magazine* ranks them
in its Top 100 in December).

By 1999, 500,000 queries a day. A new round of financing, $25 million investment from two venture capitalists (John Doerr of Kleiner Perkins and Michael Moritz of Sequoia Capital), without any loss of independence: a real Silicon Valley success story. Google moves to Mountain View, and invents Googleplex with its self-contained world and its company culture, its dogs (but not cats), its rubber balls, its twice weekly rollerblade hockey matches in the parking lot, then its cook and its masseurs, and its mobility, flexibility, informal conversations, and free time (yes, each employee is paid to work one day a week on whatever they want to in order to preserve their creativity): *mens sana in corpore sano*, and *otium ad majorem negotii gloriam*, which I write in Latin to show what a durable formula this is, even if it is hardly European any more.

They develop a new strategy analogous to that of the TV channels: They have to go and look for customers wherever they are, by authorizing other websites to add the Google search box to their own sites, and paying them three cents for every click. On June 26, 2000, they sign an agreement with Yahoo!: "Yahoo! has chosen Google because it shares our strong consumer focus," Jeff Mallett, the president of Yahoo!, said. The two companies share the same venture capitalist, Michael Moritz, both are doing their PhDs at Stanford, if I can put it like this, and Yahoo! buys eGroups from Carl Page, Larry's brother. Google by this point has indexed half a billion webpages, and is officially the number one search engine in the world. By the end of 2000, it is answering 100 million queries a day.

This considerable success as a search engine is still a long way from being a financial success. Google begins to offer targeted advertising in relation to keywords, but up until the start of 2001, it still does not have a *business model*. Google is rich in ideas, and is constantly inventing new applications (for example, Googletoolbar), but it is still poor in cash terms, and deeply in debt. Its investors are starting to get worried.

Then an Israeli entrepreneur, Yossi Vardi, enters the scene, and suggests dividing the page with a vertical line into sections: 2/3 for the search results, and 1/3 for the ads. More important, Eric Schmidt also enters the scene, imposed on Google by Moritz to keep a close eye on things, and accepted for his talents and his millions of dollars converted into shares, although not before they have made life hard for him. Schmidt is a remarkable software engineer, who challenged Microsoft's dominance with Java, was President of Novell, and with Omid Kordestani, a defector from Netscape in 1999, undertook to develop ads outside the United States. He is still chief executive officer and director, almost twenty years the senior, and twice as well paid as Brin (president of technology and director), and Page (president of products and director).[19]

On May 1, 2001, America Online (AOL, and the portal for 34 million Internet users) adopts Google as its official search engine, despite very strict conditions (several millions of dollars of financial guarantee plus stock options). On September 4, 2001, Google finally obtains its patent for PageRank. This is a key moment in its history, which we can clearly understand as a "capitalist" history and success story, with its race for cash, buyouts and mergers, competition, and plagiarism.

If Google is starting to make money, it is because it has effectively taken over the ideas of less fortunate competitors, like Bill Gross, who had already discovered everything around 1998 with GoTo.com, "everything" here being the means of financing any search with targeted advertising using keywords, and corresponding to the interest and intentions revealed by the query: This is the model of the famous *ads*[20] that claim to help rather than hinder, and to make money for the advertiser, but in actual fact make money for the middleman. Gross even prepares the ground for the way Google evolves: When a click-based payment (one cent per click) proves less profitable than anticipated for the advertiser, from 2002 only the clicks that perform count (if not with a sale, at least with a lengthy visit to a site); and keywords will be continually auctioned, so that advertisers will compete in real time, as in the market for yellow pages listed on the stock exchange ("the Yellow Pages crossed with the NASDAQ Stock Exchange," as Battelle puts it). Yet instead of renewing their agreement with GoTo, which has been renamed Overture, AOL chooses to sign an agreement with Google in 2001, since Google is making a difference thanks to PageRank, and does not mix *organic search results* with advertising, so produces the best answers. With Google, ethics pays off, and the search engine itself is organized ethically. Also GoTo/Overture, which subsequently sells to Yahoo!, takes Google to court for *patent infringement*, and Google prefers to settle high—several hundred million dollars.[21]

Google itself talks of its *love affair* with the tech community, and at the 2001 Search Engine Watch Awards, wins no less than five Oscars. Month after month acquisitions and partnerships multiply, with more and more interface languages, while new services and tools proliferate (Google News, for example, in 2002).[22] The initial public offering is delayed as long as possible, since for the time being everything is working too well for it to be in their interest to let everyone know. Brin and Page write a letter explaining their philosophy to all potential shareholders so that the IPO will happen in the most popular, populist way possible, which is not greatly appreciated by the Securities and Exchange Commission: "Google is not a conventional company. We do not intend to become one. . . . We believe a well functioning society should have abundant, free and unbiased access to high quality information. Google therefore has a responsibility to the world. The dual class structure helps ensure that this responsibility is met."[23] Since the most important aims and objectives are always to be read, like the devil, in the details of the structure, one has to understand that there are class A shares, with one vote per share, and class B shares, with ten votes per share, intended for the Google guys. Between April and August 2004 the run-up to the IPO is hard going, and full of transactions (on August 9 Yahoo! receives 2.7 million shares to prevent any further litigation) and twists and turns, with no clear sense of the implications, such as their decision to publish an interview with *Playboy* precisely during the reserve period, and which has to be appended to the Securities and Exchange Commission file.[24] On August 19 the share price rises from $15.01 to $100.01, a kind of D-Day that no doubt makes Page feel, lucky devil, that he has struck it rich. They celebrate by handing out free ice cream all day. At the start of 2006 the share price is around $460.[25]

As always, in the background, a fight to the death with Microsoft, with snatched agreements (Yahoo!, AOL), or the antitrust court case against Gates. Same thing for the data figures: On November 9, 2005, the day Microsoft is about to announce it has crawled 5 billion documents to Google's 4 billion, Google announces it has crawled 8 billion, its manifest capacity doubling in one night. Same thing for the new markets: fight to the death for the Chinese market; Yahoo! and Microsoft buy Alibaba, Google invests in Baidu (which means literally "100 times," which is still a good deal less than 10^{100} . . .); Google, say the analysts, is "Microsoft's nightmare,"[26] with the brain drain exemplified by Kai Fu Lee, hired in 1998 (the year Google was born) by Gates, founder of Microsoft Research Asia, who becomes, not without a court case, president of Google China in July 2005. On December 20, 2005, Time Warner announces that Google is buying 5 percent of shares in its subsidiary company, AOL.

This kind of saga always ends in figures, always by definition staggering, to be treated with caution, and almost immediately obsolete.[27] In 2004, 300 million queries a day. No longer 8, but 24 billion pages indexed according to the announcement in November 2005 (excluding images and Usenet messages, amounting to at least one billion for each), or 1,000 times more than when it started. Google's estimated worth in 2005 was $110 billion, more than the combined worth of Disney, the *Washington Post*, *The New York Times*, the *Wall Street Journal*, Amazon.com, Ford, and General Motors. "Historic" sales for the first trimester of 2006 of $2.25 billion (representing a growth of 79 percent relative to the same period in 2005, ahead of Yahoo! with $1.57 billion, but still a long way behind Microsoft with $11.8 billion). Profits for the trimester of $592 million (up 60 percent), a 42.7 percent market share in the United States (against

28 percent for Yahoo! and 13.2 percent for Microsoft), and 42 percent of their income outside of the United States (against 38 percent in 2005). Their profits, compared to those of Apple, IBM, or Microsoft, are still relatively weak given their quotation on the stock exchange: Brin and Page together are "worth" $22 billion in June 2005, when a share was priced at $111, and it has quadrupled since then.

So we can see how this inventive and libertarian (but equally autocratic and directive) *corporate* culture became an *incorporated* company that generated a market capitalization that most people can only dream of, in a domain whose resources, in all senses of the term, still remain largely undiscovered and underexploited.

If one were to transpose to the world of information the same asymmetry that exists between producers and consumers in the world of manufacturing, users would be akin to dumb terminals.

—Philip Agrain, *Cause Commune*

OUR MISSION IS TO ORGANIZE THE WORLD'S INFORMATION

"Our mission is to organize the world's information." "Don't be evil." Google's two big secrets of success are in principle as open and transparent as possible, since they are embodied in their two watchwords: to organize, and to do good. Respectively, organization is the PageRank algorithm that enables relevant answers to be classified, and good is the financial wizardry that enables it to accomplish its mission. Each word of these emblematic phrases is worth dwelling on at some length.

AMERICA'S SECOND MISSION

Who is this missionary "we," and what does "mission" mean?

"Our," as a possessive adjective, indicates belonging to a "we." "We," as the first person plural, includes "I" within a community. But "we," like "I," or "here" or "now," shifts reference depending on who is speaking.[1] In this case, it is "Google" who is speaking, a company that says "we," and as those of us who are teachers know all too well, accustomed as we are to reading and writing essays

40

ourselves, the "modest" we is so often almost indistinguishable from the "majestic" we. At least two interpretations immediately suggest themselves. It could be that Google is joining "us" together, one by one, in order to universalize its technological goodwill, which makes information sharing one of the new human rights. Or this "we" could be an exact reincarnation of the American "we" in the phrase "In God we trust," which features on every bill and coin.[2] In truth, it is precisely this ambiguity that is a source of anxiety; James Hadley Billington, "The Librarian," the (Republican) head of the Library of Congress, supposedly said repeatedly to his co-workers, "Anyone who is against Google is against the United States of America."

Indeed, the noun "mission" is one that is heavy with meaning, from "the sending into the world of the Son of God," to "a duty or function assumed or imposed upon a person," according to the *Oxford English Dictionary*. It is hard not to hear George Bush, magisterially concluding each of his campaign speeches with "So help me God!" in a new, quite appropriate and penetrating tone. Above all, one hears the post-9/11 "Just War," as a crusade of good against evil: "This will be a monumental struggle of good against evil, but good will prevail. Thank you very much."[3] "Don't be evil," Google's second motto, is clearly the minimal condition of possibility of such a "mission." The fact that it is an imperative, a kind of self-exhortation, and not a self-proclamation or statement, is in itself perhaps the most telling of confessions: Its transparency, it must be said, makes Google infinitely more likeable than Bush.

But it also must be said that the two missions are objectively linked to one another: Google is "America's second mission," a duty or obligation assumed alongside the "first mission" of the fight of good against evil. I see five main points of convergence between the two missions. Both have to:

1. Promote democracy ("Democracy on the Web works," we read in the section "What We Believe" on the Google homepage), and good

democracy moreover (all links are votes, but some are more equal than others).

2. Lead the war of good against evil. "Don't be evil": Bad search engines, which are bad in both senses of the word, distort their results for financial gain—whereas one has to understand, and it is enough to understand, that God/the invisible hand of the market does things well, which is to say that by encouraging good, one earns more money. Google's "goodness," which separates searching and advertising, is its best weapon in the *cyberwars*.

3. Aim to be universal. Good applies to any humanity worthy of the name ("The freedom-loving nations of the world stand by our side"),[4] and it is our mission to ensure that all are part of that humanity, "even the people in the trees," to borrow an expression from Eric Schmidt.[5]

4. Give ourselves the means over the long term. "Our response will be devastating, prolonged, effective."[6] Google's power comes from its millions of computers—the "infantrymen" who stockpile its data—and from its millions, period.

5. Take into account a shattered world. "We are dealing with a different kind of war, against a different kind of enemy. A war without battlefields or bridgeheads." The model is that of a cyberworld: One has to use the fragmentation, or network, or multitude to one's advantage— Google is intimately linked and affined to the Web.

In other words, one cannot be against—against good, against those good principles that are freedom and democracy, the right to information and the sharing of knowledge. Yet at the same time one can only be against—against a definition of good suited to a kind of interest whose definition is omitted, a particular being passed off as universal.

This shift from good with a small *g* to Good with a capital *G*, from the values of a world to the norms of the world, is called ideology.[7] Even if there is nothing more ubiquitous, one of the things a philosopher can do is to draw attention to it. Today, de facto, one cannot do without Google, just as one cannot do without America, even if both can and must evolve (or, in the case of Google, even disappear, given how technology and markets evolve—this marks a limit to the comparison between a state and a company). However, in both cases there is an analogous obscenity in passing off as moral (concerning man as man, universally) what is in fact political (concerning a human community, defined each time by its difference).[8] It is correlatively obscene to deploy economic and commercial interests in the guise of a civilizing mission. It is of course not impossible that the financial and moral coincide, but it is obscene to claim that their conjunction is more than a coincidence.

In short, the mission consists, as the section "Democracy on the Web Works" on Google's homepage proclaims, in putting order into chaos:

> Google, the end of chaos! Google search works because it relies on the millions of individuals posting links on websites to help determine which other sites offer content of value. We assess the importance of every web page using more than 200 signals and a variety of techniques, including our patented PageRank™ algorithm, which analyzes which sites have been "voted" to be the best sources of information by other pages across the web. As the web gets bigger, this approach actually improves, as each new site is another point of information and another vote to be counted.

OUR MISSION IS TO ORGANIZE

Organ, Organism, Organization: An LTI Moment

Organize: The term is analyzed by Victor Klemperer in *The Language of the Third Reich*, first published in German as *LTI: Lingua Tertii Imperii*.[9] Klemperer, a professor of French literature at the University of Dresden who was removed from his post in 1935, kept a clandestine journal that helped him to live between 1933 and 1945. In it, like Arendt and Celan, he watches as Nazism infiltrates the German language. I did not live through those dark times, but I agree with Klemperer's diagnosis: "Words can be like tiny doses of arsenic: they are swallowed unnoticed, appear to have no effect, and then after a little time the toxic reaction sets in after all" (LTI, 15–16). This, says Klemperer, is why "many words in common usage during the Nazi period should be committed to a mass grave for a very long time, some for ever" (LTI, 16). *Organize* is one of those words that makes one listen closely, and the fact that it usually does not sends shivers down my spine.

In chapter 17, "System and Organization," Klemperer explains why Nazism preferred "organization" to "system": "A system is something which is 'assembled,' a construction, a structure built by hands and tools according to the dictates of reason." So one talks of "railway systems" or the "Kantian system." As he goes on to say, "for Kant—for the professional, trained philosopher one might say—to philosophize means to think systematically. And it is this very way of thinking which the National Socialist rejects from the innermost core of his being, which he despises out of a desire for self-preservation" (LTI, 98). "If the word system is frowned upon," asks Klemperer, "how does the Nazi system of government refer to itself? Because they have a system as well, after all, and are proud of the fact that absolutely every expression and situation in life is caught up in this network; that is why 'totality' [*Totalität*] is one of the foundations on which the LTI is built. They don't have a *System*, they have an *Organization*, they don't think systematically with the power of reason, they cull secrets from all that is organic" (LTI, 98–99).

I read several important interconnected elements here.

First of all, the link between totality and organization. If I apply this to Google, the two key terms are "to organize all . . . in the world." Which is why I have one immediate piece of advice for any digital library past, present, and future: systematize, do not organize, make a distinction between a "system," an ensemble arranged with discernment and intelligence, which holds together (*sunistēmi*), and an "organization," which links the organic to instrumentality. And it is quite strange, even in the Greek, logic is an *organon*, and the hand is, according to Aristotle's definition, the organ of organs, that is, the instrument capable of replacing or of using all instruments. In Greek, there are two ways of saying "whole": *pan* and *holon*, an open composite whole or a closed totality. When we are talking about information, the whole is necessarily a *pan* connected to the infinite, that is, to the "more and more"—the infinite in its Aristotelian definition, depreciative, privative (or bad infinity, as it will subsequently become in the history of philosophy): not that outside of which there is nothing more, but that outside of which there is always something else. One + one piece of information, ad infinitum, adjoining each one to the next in time, in a linear time, with neither dialectic nor eternal return of the same, as befits an expanding infinity. No *Aufhebung* (no "sublation" or "overcoming" as it is sometimes translated) of information is possible. The will to information is always the will to more information, by analogy with the will to power. Google's vocation is a *panic* response, intimately linked to the Web as an expanding universe. One might tentatively suggest the following difference: The whole in a state of "panic" does not itself constitute a system; it expands organically. But a "holistic" library would not be the organization of all information, rather a provisional system of culture, to the extent that could, at least partially, systematize its flaws and gaps.

Second, the idea of naturalization. Klemperer, as a Hellenist, underlines the way in which Alfred Rosenberg "finally enthrone[s] the notion of the 'organic'": "in Greek, *orgaō* means to swell, to put out shoots, to be trained unconsciously, like a plant" (LTI, 99). Organization is something technical passing itself off as something natural, the naturalization of technique. This is precisely the definition of PageRank, which expresses the "reality of the network": The secret of the organic in the organization called Google is the secret of the technical—the network, the computer: "No humans are reading the email, just Google's systems." The Web is an organism, with a natural self-organization (Web self-organizing properties), exactly like the invisible hand of the market: "It happens naturally as a response to queries."[10]

Consequently, one cannot help but internalize this hierarchy, in the same way one adopts a language: "As early as 1936, a young car mechanic who had managed to carry out a tricky emergency repair on my exhaust all by himself said to me, 'Didn't I organize that well!' The words *'Organisation'* and *'Organisieren'* [to organize] were ringing in his ears so insistently . . . that he couldn't even come up with an appropriate and simple expression like *arbeiten* [to work], *erledigen* [to deal with], or *verrichten* [to carry out] or even just *machen* [to do] for a task which he himself undertook and completed" (LTI, 101–102). "*Organisieren* was a benign word which had become fashionable everywhere, it was the most commonplace expression to describe an activity which had itself become commonplace. . . . For some time now I have been writing: it was . . . it was. But who was it who said only yesterday: 'I must organize some tobacco for myself?' I fear it was me" (LTI, 102).

PageRank, or the Self-Organizing System
The algorithm

What exactly is PageRank?

The answer is found once again on Google's early homepage:

> The main element of our software is PageRank, a system of classifying Web pages developed by the founders of Google . . . at Stanford University. And while dozens of IT engineers and specialists spend their days improving different aspects of Google, PageRank remains the cornerstone of our search engine.[11]

We know that 80 percent of searches stop at the first page and that they rarely go further than the third page. "Tomorrow, what is not available online is in danger of becoming invisible globally," said Jacques Chirac,[12] but nowadays, whatever does not appear in the first results of a Google search has very little existence. PageRank is the ranking system whose exclusive license, it is worth repeating, was awarded to Google by Stanford University only until 2011. It is a secret formula, as secret apparently as that of Coca-Cola, which it is said contains 500 million variables and more than 2 billion terms.[13]

$$W_j = (1-d) + d \sum_{i=1, i \neq j}^{N} l_{i,j} \frac{W_i}{n_i}$$

Actual PageRank model

One can, however, find its algorithm on the Internet. (See the accompanying illustration.)

It is a Markov chain.[14] I learn from Wikipedia that a Markov chain is a stochastic process whereby the prediction of the future from the present does not require knowledge of the past (Arendt, quoting René Char: "Our heritage is left to us by no testament" [*Notre héritage n'est précédé d'aucun testament*]). A good example of this, besides Brownian motion, is the way in which I can predict the behavior of Doudou the hamster: eating, sleeping, running on his exercise wheel (or as the French say, *métro, boulot, dodo*—subway, work, sleep). Freedom is always the ignorance of the causes that make us act, as Spinoza puts it.

"The Anatomy of a Large-Scale Hypertextual Web Search Engine" gives an intuitive justification for the *d* parameter, or the weighting factor. It corresponds to the probability that the random surfer gets bored and visits a new random page. But the decisive factor of the equation is the number of links that lead to a page, the value of these links being itself the object of a weighting.[15]

The academic model

The basic idea that Brin and Page have, in order to classify and hierarchize the relevance of results, and which Vise calls a "one-shot idea,"[16] is to take into consideration not only the keywords that determine a site but also the links that are directed toward it. The anatomy of the large search engine backs onto, so to speak, the idea of a *back rub*, or of *back links*, that is, links that lead to the site and not that go out from it, so as to correct the failings of previous search engines.[17]

In "Anatomy," the two doctoral students give an excellent description of the "academic" concepts PageRank was based upon: "At the same time, search engines have migrated from the academic domain to the commercial. . . . With Google, we have a strong goal to push more development and understanding into the academic realm." Page starts out from the idea that the entire Web has as its premise citation (the link) and annotation (the description of the link). The relationship between a search engine and the world of research is thus identified at the same time as a very "academic" definition of the world of research: quotation, annotation, authority, peer evaluation, classification, and even the idea of what a bad essay is, as a perverse effect of the educational system. A bad essay is stuffed full of quotations, and the more of them there are, the less likely they are to be good references: The more links a site creates, the less valuable the link emanating from this site will be.

This is nothing new, but what is new is the way in which they took the bull by the horns. The idea was already contained in the invention of the World Wide Web by Tim Berners-Lee in 1991, who describes it as follows: "The project started out with the philosophy that academic information should largely be accessible for all. The WWW consists of documents and links. Indices are particular kinds of documents that are not so much the object of a reading as of a search. The result of a search of this kind is another ("virtual") document that contains links leading to the documents found."[18] It is all there: academic information, free open access for all, links and indexation—all except for the algorithm itself.

The problem is essentially the following, as diagnosed in the "Anatomy": how to use the Web, which is "a vast collection of completely heterogeneous documents," as if it were one or more "well controlled collections"? This is a problem for any librarian, a problem of bibliometrics, and it comes as no surprise that Brin and Page should be interested in Jon Kleinberg, who suggests evaluating the "authoritative sources in a hyperlink environment" with the help of the *Garfield impact factor*: in short, the weighted number of citations. One can finally quantify value via the citation or the link.

With PageRank, Google is merely showing what happens to

everyone everywhere. The hierarchy depends on the objective manifestation of how highly one regards something. This is very concretely how World Rankings work. For example, in 2005 "Shanghai," which is the ranking used by the University of Shanghai to determine where it sends its students, to our shame had the first French university, Paris VI, at number 46 (down five places), Paris XI at number 61 (down thirteen places), while the ENS Rue d'Ulm was at number 93, right after Strasbourg I.[19] The CNRS, which is an atypical organization (it was set up by Léon Blum along the lines of the unusual model of the Academy of Sciences in Russia), does not even make an appearance. The ranking works by integrating a certain number of strictly defined criteria, among them the citation index, that is, the number of times a researcher has been cited in a prescribed corpus of journals.[20] And just as with Google, if you notice you have a low ranking, you can try to improve it and do better next time. The winning system, so long as the rules do not change, is for "us" a question of publishing in English on important subjects, within an institutional grouping that constitutes a critical mass with a distinctive identity, expressing paradoxical opinions against which researchers in the field will be required to position themselves positively or negatively (it matters little, so long as it is quoted), in the most prestigious journals within a given corpus. It is necessary, and sufficient, to take the instrument of control as the objective of one's activity. The world of finance calls this "signaling theory." Research becomes what the journals say research is, and researchers only exist henceforth as bureaucrats.[21]

Quality as an emergent property of quantity, or doxa *squared*

"PageRank is a champion of democracy": Its procedures are assimilated to universal suffrage, but weighted by an aristocracy of importance by means of analyzing content, according to a mixed model of enlightened or well-tempered democracy:

> PageRank is a champion of democracy: it takes advantage of the innumerable links on the Web to evaluate the content of Web

pages, and their relevance to the search. The principle of PageRank is simple: every link from page A indicating page B is considered as a vote by page A for page B. However, Google does not limit its evaluation to the number of "votes" (links) received per page: it also goes on to analyze the content of the link. The links present in pages deemed important by Google have more "weight" and thus contribute to "electing" other pages.[22]

So:

1. One link, one vote (not *one man, one vote*, as in South Africa).
2. All links are not equivalent: The number of citations is weighted according to the value of the site.
3. The value of the site and of the citation (of the "sitation," one might say) is itself measured by the number of links that refer to it, the most important site being the one to which most sites or links refer (for Google, a mention on the first page of Yahoo! is priceless).

Quality is thus nothing other than an emergent property of quantity. Hierarchy does not come from outside, like a Platonic hierarchy dictated by having to be of need, with a philosopher-king to impose it upon the masses, and nor is it a democratic hierarchy by *agōn*, or open discussion, dissension, and consensus. It is immanent, because "we" are the only ones to practice it, and yet it remains opaque because it is mechanical and robotic, mathematical and systemic.

Importance within the domain of opinion is the measure of the importance of the opinion. In ancient Greek, the *doxa* is squared, and in Marxist terms, you only lend to the rich (capital creates capital). Originality, atypicality, genius, or the singularity and untimeliness of the truth do not form part of the system unless they are made commonplace: There is no otherness to *doxa*. It is "opinion" that is the point of departure and the point of arrival, the measure and the criterion. It defines the ontological status of the objects that are on the web, and of the ranking Google gives them.[23]

BOX D

What is *doxa*?

Doxa, from *dokeō*, "to appear" or "to seem" (from the same family as *dekomai*, "to receive, welcome, accept," cf. Latin *decet*) is for us one of the most polysemic words in Greek. *Doxa* unites what has been split apart between a subjective sense (what one expects, what one believes, what one thinks is good) and an objective sense (what appears, what is apparent, what seems). The spectrum of meanings in each case contains a full and extreme range of values, from the most negative to the most positive, from hallucination ("false opinion, imagination, conjecture") to the normative accuracy of an accepted idea ("expectation, estimation, conjecture, belief, dogma, reputation"), and from deceptive appearance ("illusion, false appearance") to apparition in all its splendor ("phenomenon, glory"). The common translation of *doxa* by "opinion" could never encompass this whole range of meanings, of course.

Doxa has been constantly rethought and reappropriated from one system to the next, and as such, it reveals in a sense the history of philosophy. It all begins with Parmenides. The goddess who shows the path to follow begins with the opposition *alētheia/doxa*, "truth, opinion," in order to structure what she unveils: " 'Tis necessary for thee to learn all things, both the abiding essence of persuasive truth (*alētheiēs*), and men's opinions (*doxa*) in which rests no true belief" (I, 28–30). Plato, in *The Republic*, develops a systematic opposition between "science" (*epistē mē*), which applies to being and knows it as it is, and "opinion", which is applied "neither to that which is nor that which is not" (478c), but deals with "something between the two" (478d). The opposition is structured as the separation between the intelligible world and the sensible world:

thus "philosophers" consider "beauty itself," while the mass of "philodoxers" are solely content to contemplate "beautiful colors" (480a).

The Aristotelian reinterpretation of *doxa* involves reevaluating this world, the individual, the contingent, the probable, the persuasive, the common. It may be true that science, through definition and demonstration, can only deal with the universal and the necessary: this may be true, but this is to say, positively, that *doxa* deals with the individual and the "each and every" "that it is opinion (*doxa*) that deals with that which can be otherwise than as it is" (*Metaphysics*, Zeta, 15, 1039b 34–1040a I). Aristotle is terminologically innovative in using the word *endoxon* (literally "that which is in, *en*, the *doxa*) to refer to the "premises conforming to opinion" which are used to produce dialectical syllogisms, as distinct from scientific or demonstrative syllogisms. And he defines *endoxa*, as distinct from "true and first" propositions, as "what is received [*ta dokounta*] by all or by the greatest number, or by the wise [*sophois*], and, among the latter, either by all or by the greatest number, or by the best known and the most reputable [*endoxois*]" (100b 21–23). We can see how *ta endoxa*, likely premises or received ideas, imply the *doxa* of *endoxoi*, the opinion of illustrious men. We can also therefore understand that Aristotle's treatises begin by reminding us of opinions, which constitute the history of the discipline, and that doxography, or literally "writing of opinions," becomes an entirely separate and distinct genre. Aristotle thus returns to Heraclitus, who, far more critically, based *dokeonta*, well-known things, on the renown of the most reputable, *ho dokimōtatos*, who is really nothing other than a guardian of the *doxa*, or strictly speaking, someone who conserves, a "conservationist. "The best known decides on the things that are known, which he conserves" (fr. 28).

Human knowledge, insofar as it is information that is conveyed and used and serves as a point of departure for common and persuasive constructions, is of the order of opinion and not of truth. This is in effect the "ontological" status of the classification of information we find on Google, which is intimately linked and affined to the status of information as such.

This is a serious charge, philosophically speaking. With PageRank we are, for better or for worse, in the domain of rhetoric, of commonplaces (Wikipedia's *uncontroversial topics*). For better: The ideas that are accepted, by the greatest number and by the most renowned people, constitute our common world—we find the same weighting of democracy by aristocracy in Aristotle as we do in Page-Rank. For worse: When the common world produces only "clichés," and when we are unthinkingly bogged down in what Hannah Arendt calls the "banality of evil," not so much because evil is banal, but rather because it becomes impossible to say or live anything other than banalities.

"Your Query": The Customer and His/Her Customs

There are two elements to page ranking. The first, PageRank, corresponds to what Google calls the "reality of the Web," which is the objective component. The second is "you," the subjective component. "You," a personal pronoun that floats deictically between singular and plural, in the same way that it does in the most quintessential of political slogans: "You are the majority." This time "our mission," that is Google's mission, is to ensure the ranking responds to "your query."

The sites which stand out in terms of their quality are assigned a higher PageRank value, and Google takes this into account when searching. Of course, the pages Google judges to be "important" are going to leave you indifferent if they do not respond to your search . . . So in order to find the pages which best correspond to your search, Google supplements the PageRank evaluation with highly developed text correspondence mechanisms. It is not enough for Google just to count the number of occurrences of a search term in a page: it examines different aspects of the content of this page (and of the content of pages linked to it) in order to determine whether or not it corresponds to your query.[24]

From this point of view, the essential value of a result is its *relevance*. *Relevance* is an excellent translation of the Greek *prepon*, a key term in rhetoric: the state of being adapted or appropriate to the expectation of the audience (including what is "suitable," in Latin *decorum*, from *decet*, which gives us "decency"). The entire secret algorithm is driven by *prepon*, and the ultimate *prepon* involves adapting the offer to the demand.

You are given what you ask for, so you are only given what you are in a position to ask for. You would not search for me if you had not already found me: I would maintain that the market, like faith, is the exact opposite of education. It is true that the Web is a space for the curious, one can wander around in Google the same way one can walk among the bookshelves in a library, or rather in a department store. But the excellence of Google is in shortening your search time, and preventing your wandering around Google can teach you how to ask, so that your search is more appropriate to the way in which the search engine works, and so that you find the answers that interest you more quickly, but it cannot, nor does it want to, teach you about what you want, or the things you are interested in, but which it depends upon to give you greater satisfaction.

In order to do this, it banks on your habits, according to a behaviorist technique of identification and profiling.

On your first visit to the Google site, Google installs a cookie on your computer. A cookie is a small unit of data that gives you a unique identification. At Google, we use cookies to improve the quality of our services, and to analyze better our user base.

The method used is as follows: Google records user preferences in these cookies, and analyses their behavior during searches. Google is committed to never communicating the content of these cookies to third parties—except when legally required to do so, such as for a search warrant, a court appearance, a judicial decision, etc.

Please take a cookie: as innocent as Google itself, of the same mental age (7–77 years), and universal in its humor. No one is forcing you, but it is for your own good. Just as it is for the general good that you will be reported to the authorities if the law demands it.[25]

In their default settings most web browsers accept cookies. You can modify the settings and refuse all cookies, or ask for a message to be displayed every time a site tries to install a cookie (with the possibility of choosing Yes or No). You should, however, be aware that by refusing cookies, you block certain functions of Google's search services.

You have the option of saying no at any time, except that you have to say so: The politics of the forced hand is simply a matter of automating one of two alternative choices, obviously "the best."[26] We should mobilize against the notion that "silence is consent": Silence is simply not speaking.

Whichever way you look at it, Google is always helping you to perfect your needs, to be yourself, whether by suggesting the usual spelling ("search instead for . . ."), or your previous searches, or by analyzing your behavior as a customer and deducing what you want. The *clickstream* enables Google to personalize the most fitting response, to adapt it to you. It records an ID number on your hard drive, as indelible and identifying as the "ITIN" number, it *customizes* you. A *customer*, as its name implies, is someone who is known by his or her "customs," or habits, or ethos: He or she becomes a regular visitor. On can better understand now the link between marketing, profiling, and ethics, as well as the link between marketing and addiction: Google is a drug, and we will see with their financial wizardry how profitable this all becomes.[27] In the meantime, if you have anything to hide, dispose of your computer after using it, and change computers frequently. You will be much harder to track down, since cookies will remain in your computer until 2038, and the information within the cookie, and about you, are stored indefinitely.

Google's triumph is down to the fact that, on the one hand, it enables the greatest objectivity or impartiality. It is the system, and the system alone, that produces the order of results: Your search is determined by everything you have previously searched for. It is "pure," and without commercial bias. On the other hand, it allows for the greatest subjectivity or adaptability to an individual search: It responds to your search, to your usage as a user, to the kinds of desires that characterize you personally. The only bias is "you." The winning formulas of organization are naturalization and adaptation.

THE WORLD'S INFORMATION

Google organizes information. What is information, and is there anything else besides information?

To Inform, Information, Information Technology

Informatio, from *informo*, or to put into form (to "present" and to "imagine") means "conception, explanation" and "sketch" in Latin. In French, according to the *Dictionnaire historique de la langue française*, the first attested meaning is juridical: "criminal investigation," later "information obtained from someone," and then around 1500 (but rarely before the twentieth century), "all of the knowledge on something gathered together." This is the usual meaning nowadays, and it is linked to the development of the press (cf. Zola in 1886), or to be more exact, information brought to the attention of the public. Moreover the French *information*, "borrowed from the meaning of the English 'information' (around 1950) is a specialist term used to refer to an element or a system that is transmissible by a signal or a combination of signals (information theory)." This is where the French *informatique* [information technology or science] comes from, a term created by Philippe Dreyfus in 1962 on the model of *mathématique* [mathematics], *électronique* [electronics], and so on. The word refers to "the science and the entire range of automated techniques relating to information (data collection, memory storage, usage, etc.) and the economic activity applying this science and these techniques." The *Dictionnaire culturel* even gives the quotation by Dreyfus, taken from an interview with Philippe Breton: "The resulting word brought together information and automatic, *infor . . . matique*, it is as clear as that."[28] The *Dictionnaire historique de la langue française* concludes: "*Informatique* is related to notions of order (cf. *ordinateur*, computer), or data storage . . . of information," and it reminds us of the definition of cybernetics (*cybernétique*) in 1948 by its founding father, Norbert Wiener.[29] "The study of the processes of control and communication in living beings and machines" indeed associates effective life with adequate information: "To live effectively is to live with adequate information. Information is the name for the content of what is exchanged with the outer world as we adjust to it, and make our adjustment felt upon it."[30]

The explicit horizon of the contemporary notion of information, even if we have forgotten it, is a behaviorism supported by a feedback loop.

Information, Knowledge, and Culture
A knowledge-based society

What is a world in which there is only information, in which knowledge and culture are only apprehended as information?[31] It is not self-evident to equate these three terms. Google uses and makes us use this equivalence as if it were self-evident: "Is your goal to have the entire world's knowledge connected directly to our minds?"[32] *Playboy* asks Brin. His answer is: "To get closer to that—as close as possible."

"We" accept this usage. This equivalence functions constantly, particularly in all of the defining texts of the society that "we" constitute, that grey literature written by and for Europe. A *knowledge-based society* is how the European Union defines itself and today's world: The phrase is repeated so often that we think we understand it. This is what we read on the Knowledge Society homepage of the European Commission:

> to become the most competitive and dynamic knowledge-based economy in the world, capable of sustainable economic growth with more and better jobs and greater social cohesion (strategic goal for 2010 set for Europe at the Lisbon European Council, March 2000).[33]
>
> The fast development of Information and Communications Technology (ICT) has brought about deep changes in our way of working and living, as the widespread diffusion of ICT is accompanied by organizational, commercial, social and legal innovations.
>
> Our society is now defined as the "Information Society," a society in which low-cost information and ICT are in general use, or as the "Knowledge(-based) Society," to stress the fact that the most valuable asset is investment in tangible, human and social capital and that the key factors are knowledge and creativity.

We see here a clear equivalence between knowledge society and information society, and even the suggestion that society and economy are substitutable (French: "*société de la connaissance*"; English: "knowledge-based economy"). Knowledge presupposes the diffusion of this knowledge, which is why it can be reduced to, or confused with information. In theory, this is a good goal: to leave no one behind, to work against a digitally fractured society. In practice, it is quite serious, since it confuses information and culture under the heading of *knowledge*. Or to put it differently, it confuses curiosity and astonishment, the *thaumas* that Aristotle referred to as the cause of man's natural desire to know, the source of the love of knowledge that is philosophy.

The excellent, balanced and well-informed article by Jean-Michel Salaün on "Digital libraries and Google Print" is important in this regard. He notes: "'Google's mission is to organize the world's information with the goal of making it accessible and useful to all': so begins the introduction to the company on its website. Is this not precisely the mission of a global library devoted to the general interest?"[34] While he points out the paradox—a private operator collects without constraints, whereas a public operator proposes selection criteria—he does not call into question the concept of "information" as it applies to culture or libraries.[35] From now on, culture will be nothing more than well-organized information, whose reliability is guaranteed.

Another model: The artwork

The definition of culture as reliable information is one we ought to refuse. "For these reasons any discussion of culture must somehow take as its starting point the phenomenon of art," says Hannah Arendt,[36] and she proposes an entirely different way of envisaging culture. An object, she says, is cultural by virtue of its permanence and its mode of appearance ("for the sole purpose of appearance"; *CC*, 210). This is why she sets up an opposition between what she calls the "cultured philistine" (CC, 20) and the entertainment industry: The former evaluates and devalues "cultural things into social commodities" (CC, 205), the latter "consumes" (CC, 205), that is to say, ingests, digests, and renders them invisible as things. The risk, obviously, is that we all recognize ourselves in both one and the other. Indeed, this is the "crisis in culture" to which Arendt refers, and the reason why she often sounds rather grumpy to our Google-acclimatized ears.

However, I would like to pursue her analysis for a while. The trouble with the philistine, according to Arendt, is that "the great works of art are no less misused when they serve purposes of self-education or self-perfection than when they serve any other purposes" (CC, 203). Arendt is quite radical here: "It may be as useful and legitimate to look at a picture in order to perfect one's knowledge of a given period as it is useful and legitimate to use a painting in order to hide a hole in the wall" (CC, 203). So much for the relationship between culture and knowledge (or at least a certain type of knowledge). The cultured philistine, you and me, is certainly a Google enthusiast. Google, and its academic model, turn out to belong to Europe's past, to an irresistibly outmoded nineteenth century!

As for mass society, what it does is to consume. As long as it only consumes what it creates, all is well: "we can no more reproach it for the non-durability of its articles than we can reproach a bakery because it produces goods which, if they are not to spoil, must be consumed as soon as they are made" (CC, 206). In this respect, entertainment is less of a threat to society than "educational gadgets" (CC, 207). However, "mass culture comes into being when mass society seizes upon cultural objects, and its danger is that the life process of society . . . will literally consume the cultural objects, eat them up and destroy them" (CC, 207).

Arendt tries to distinguish between mass society and "mass distribution": "When books and pictures in reproduction are thrown on the market cheaply and sold in vast quantities, this does not affect the nature of the objects in question. But their nature is affected when these objects themselves are changed—rewritten, condensed, digested, reduced to kitsch in reproduction, or in preparation for the movies. This does not mean that culture spreads to the masses, but that culture is being destroyed in order to yield entertainment" (CC, 207). However, she does finally recognize that mass culture as such does not exist: "The result is, of course, not mass culture which, strictly speaking, does not exist, but mass entertainment, feeding on the cultural objects of the world. To believe that such a society will become more 'cultured' as time goes on and education has done its work is, I think, a fatal mistake. The point is that a consumer society cannot possibly know how to take care of a world and the things which belong exclusively to the space of worldly appearances, because its central attitude towards all objects, the attitude of consumption, spells ruin to everything it touches" (CC, 211).

I am very interested in understanding why her position is literally untenable today. On the one hand, how can we claim that the "reproduction," of a painting for example, or of a book on the Web, does not "affect" its nature? Are we not then dealing with another work of art, another kind of work, or even something other than a work of art? But on the other hand, how could we tolerate being politically incorrect to the point of being, purely and simply, against mass distribution? She is thus trapped in a circular argument, but she does see and say the essential thing: that culture is characterized not by knowledge, nor by information, but by works of art and by taste. It all comes down ultimately to a question of "choice": "A cultivated person ought to be: one who knows how to choose his company among men, among thoughts, in the present as well as in the past" (CC, 226). As she says earlier, "Could it be that taste belongs among the political faculties?" (CC, 215).

One might claim that the model of the work of art and the author is reshaped with cyberculture, and that it is once and for all outmoded, just as it is in art. Even if I do not share this opinion—since I believe in untimeliness rather than obsolescence—it is obviously not enough, for cyberculture to have any meaning, to conceive of the author differently, as "collective" or anonymous, nor to conceive of the spectator as an interactive participant, and a quasi-author: For this reason, we need to conceive of the work of art in another way. I do not see that thinking of it as information is sufficient; we have to think of it rather as performance.[37] *Energeia* rather than *ergon*, a work-in-progress rather than a finished work of art, and we thus come back (itself a proof against obsolescence) to what Humboldt says about language being the *collective work* par excellence.

Order, ordination, computer (ordinateur), or the
incomparable (and unstoppable) essence of Google

Google reveals the Internet: Google's incomparable essence comes from how well matched it is to the Web, to information technology, and even to the computer.

The *Dictionnaire historique de la langue française* tells us that *ordinateur*, contrary to popular linguistic sentiment, is an ancient word. *Ordinator* refers to the person who regulates, who puts order into something and, in Christian Latin, the person who is responsible for an ordination, like the *ordonnateur* [organizer] of a ceremony, the director, or the person in charge overall. It goes on to say that contemporary usage has given rise to a "homonym," that is, the *ordinateur* in the domain of information technology, "where the word was formed according to the original meaning in Latin, 'to put into order,' replacing the English word *computer*, which privileges the idea of calculation, at the request of IBM France in 1954. *Ordinateur*, against all the odds, has won out over the Anglicism *computer*, and its French adaptation *computeur*." When the *Dictionnaire culturel* quotes Jacques Perret, in a letter to IBM dated April 16, 1955, one might wonder whether it really is a case of homonymy:

> "What would you think of *ordinateur? It is a well formed word . . . like the adjective referring to God who puts order into the world.* A word of this kind has the advantage of easily becoming a verb, *ordiner,* and a noun describing the action, *ordination.* The disadvantage is that *ordination* refers to a religious ceremony: but the two areas of meaning (religion and accounting) are so far apart . . . that the disadvantage is perhaps insignificant" (my emphasis).

One might also believe, since Weber, that the distance between religion and accounting is in fact one of denial, and one might find in the God of Leibniz the necessary and sufficient middle term allowing us to move from the order of reason and of divine computation to the portable computer, with which each monad is harmonically equipped these days. Harmony, after all, happens by itself with Google.

For what does a computer do? It transforms quantity—because it is discreet, either nothing or something, 0 or 1—into quality, that is, singular and differentiated information. Using the principle of reason (why is there something rather than nothing?), and the principle of indiscernibles that is deduced from it, it creates a universal binary characteristic such that two distinct entities are never represented by the same sequence. So Leibniz, and his monads generating a singular chain of predicates, could be seen as the basis of Turing's great invention.

This transformation of quantity into quality, which accounts for the way in which a computer works, also accounts for Google's constitutive equation, PageRank, as we have seen. The number of links and the number of clicks, which are discreet quantities, are the basis of the quality and of the value of the information provided: They inform this information.

Discreet quantity is sufficient because time does not count in the way it counts for humans. Breaking everything down into "characters" can take a very long time for us (even though it is not infinitely long), but it is very short in machine time, and given that there is not an infinite number of simultaneous clicks, machine "memory" is sufficient. At every instant (t), information is located on a row (R), whatever it may be.

This is what I call the unstoppable essence of Google: the fact that quantity is essentially sufficient for quality, that is to say, singularity.

4

DON'T BE EVIL

Today the spirit of religious asceticism—whether finally, who knows?—has escaped from the cage. . . . No one knows who will live in this cage in the future, or whether at the end of this tremendous development entirely new prophets will arise, or there will be a great rebirth of old ideas and ideals, or, if neither, mechanized petrification, embellished with a sort of convulsive self-importance.

—Max Weber, *The Protestant Ethic and the Spirit of Capitalism*

We have to do better on every search in every language everywhere in the world.

—Eric Schmidt, Washington University, May 2005

Google, combined with wifi, is a little bit like God. God is wireless, God is everywhere and God sees and knows everything. Throughout history, people connected to God without wires.

—Thomas L. Friedman, *New York Times*

GOOGLE IS GOOD, PROVIDED IT IS NOT EVIL!

PLAYBOY: Is your company motto really "Don't be evil"?

BRIN: Yes, it's real.

PLAYBOY: Is it a written code?

BRIN: Yes. We have other rules, too.

PAGE: We allow dogs, for example.

BRIN: As for "Don't be evil," we have tried to define precisely what it
        means to be a force for good—always do the right, ethical thing.
        Ultimately, "Don't be evil" seems the easiest way to summarize it.

PAGE: Apparently people like it better than "Be good."

BRIN: It's not enough not to be evil. We also actively try to be good.

PLAYBOY: Who ultimately decides what is evil? Eric Schmidt, your CEO,
        once said, "Evil is whatever Sergey decides is evil."

PAGE: That was not one of his best quotes, though it's memorable."[1]

The rest of the interview gives us quite haphazardly, but in all se-
riousness, the reasons why Google is good: "Google is all about getting the right information to people quickly, easily, cheaply—and
for free. We serve the world—all countries, at least 100 different languages. It's a powerful service that most people probably couldn't
have dreamed of 20 years ago. It's available to the rich, the poor,
street children in Cambodia, stock traders on Wall Street—basically
everybody. It's very democratic."

Freedom, equality, availability: a dream come true. At first glance,
it is true. "We" who all use Google know it. *Free* from the *land of
the free*, again and always affine to the essence of the Web. We truly
should say "Bravo" and "Thank you." How is it possible, though, to
offer such an inherently costly service for free? A second analysis
will allow us to interpret its negative form, and to reframe its democratic ambition.

Just like Bartleby's *"I would prefer not to,"* "don't be evil" is a
matter of negotiation. I propose summarizing in the following way
(adopting or adapting a mix of Leibniz and Spinoza, who are a priori incompatible):

1. Google is good. It produces the best of all possible worlds by ensuring that the minimum amount of inevitable evil is turned, according to a principle of global economics, to the advantage of the maximum amount of good. In other words, the money generated by advertising allows even more information to be made available to even more people.

2. Every monad, or every connected individual, is itself a part of Google. We have seen how each individual's behavior is stored through PageRank in the continuous operation forming the evolving whole that is the Internet. This accounts for the extraordinary success of Google manuals and advisors explaining how to modify PageRank to make one's "immanence" on the Web work to one's advantage; as Page says in the *Playboy* interview, "it's like discovering fire: 'We can affect the Web!' Well *you are the Web*, so of course you can affect it" (my emphasis). But this also accounts for the moral imperative: Every one of "us" must, just like Google, choose to be good, which is to say, let Google/the Web play freely and without bias. And if we are not good, and we end up getting caught red-handed, we will be punished through the means by which we have sinned.

3. While this self-organization may be purely immanent, it is accompanied by the possibility, clearly visible in Google's charter, of sudden transcendence, of a "miracle," as proof of the existence of a God, who this time is well and truly transcendent. The Web is "us," but this time, "we" are not the same as "you":

> *We* reserve the right to change or discontinue our services as
> necessary, for whatever reason, and without notice, including
> the right to discontinue services with or without notice, without
> incurring any liability towards *you*, or any other user, or any other
> third party. We reserve the right to change the present terms and
> conditions as necessary and without notice; to be informed about
> these possible changes, we recommend that you regularly reread
> these terms and conditions.[2]

But provided God is not evil, everything will be for the best in the best of all possible worlds, will it not?

FINANCIAL WIZARDRY, OR HOW THE MISSION MAKES MONEY
In the Margins: Ads, or Trading in Words

Google's financial wizardry is very simple, and all the more admirable because of its simplicity. Although it claims to refuse any advertising, Google pulls in between 96 percent and 99 percent of its revenue (depending on the source, or how you count it) from advertising. It is becoming de facto the place where global commerce is negotiated. After having tried to sell itself as a search engine (that is, as a licensing business), it turned to self-financing through advertising (as an advertising business).[3] But instead of directly selling a space in the results page displayed to the highest bidder, as its competitors do, Google simply sells ads and marginal mentions. Its "pure," free searches are thus financed in the margins, in all senses of the term, through advertising.

These ads are words. Google trades in words. Advertisers buy one or more keywords (which Google's keyword generator can moreover help them to choose), and their ad, containing the link to their site, will appear on each query containing this keyword. One can see how much the language of Google/the Web is essentially a language of keywords: It is keywords that on the one hand define information and on the other hand are bought and sold. Information is thus a "sophisticated 24-hour marketplace where thousands of words and phrases that people search for every day were bought and sold like goods and services."[4] "Pet food" costs thirty cents, but "investment advice" costs three dollars! The keyword market takes place in real time, just like in the stock exchange, or at an auction, since there are a limited number of spaces for each keyword, and then each portfolio of words is managed (the plural "digital cameras" is more expensive than the singular, since buyers who want to compare click on the plural, whereas the majority of curious

browsers click on the singular). One of the most expensive words
has been "mesothelioma," a type of cancer caused by exposure to
asbestos, which a group of lawyers were dealing with.

Advertisers can choose to pay per click. Everything is for the best
in the best of all possible worlds: Advertisers advertise where they
have the best chance of finding customers, and they pay only when
potential customers are there. Customers sees a visibly sponsored
ad, which they can choose to ignore, but this ad, unlike TV ads which
interrupt a show (what Patrick Le Lay, director general of France's
TF1, famously referred to as "available brain time"), is most likely to
interest customers without annoying them, and Google earns one
cent per click:

> Ads with Google AdWords allow you to reach new prospective
> customers at the exact moment they are searching for your
> products or services.
>
> Google AdWords offers you the possibility of creating your ads
> and of choosing the keywords that will help us target your
> customers. You are only billed when users click on your ads.
>
> Google AdWords allows you to reach internet users when they are
> searching for your products or services. Your website thus records
> visits from potential targeted customers. The cost per click (CPC)
> pricing means that you only pay when users click on your ads.

After AdWords for advertisers, between March and June 2003
Google created AdSense for website editors, whereby for a payment
they agree to allow Google to relay ads related to the content of
their website.

> Generate more income from your website by providing the online
> services and information most useful to your visitors. Google
> AdSense automatically sends out text-based and image-based
> ads, targeted exactly at your website and its content. These ads
> are so relevant that they offer additional useful information to
> your visitors. And if you add the Google Search function on your

website, Google AdSense also sends out targeted ads on your results pages. Google AdSense allows you to increase your income with a minimum of effort, and without any additional cost.[5]

Battelle explains very well the connection to Google's acquisition of Blogger: With blogs, Google has developed a formidable network of advertisers who "only have to add a few lines of code to their website, then sit back and watch as checks sent by Google arrive in their letter boxes a few months later." Even if AdSense does not work as well as AdWords, it is the simplicity of the setup, along with its hardware, which makes it so robust.

Virtue at Every Stage

Let us recap the different stages of virtue, which always comes under the two headings of relevance and respect for the "reality of the Web."

1. Google, unlike Yahoo!, does not mix search and advertising— it is a kind of separation of church and state.[6]

This is already evident at the level of presentation. Just as the homepage is always minimalist (the logo, the central window, and the suggestions, and most important, nothing but text, with occasional exceptions), the answer display makes a very clear distinction on the page between the search results (*free search*) and the commercial links (*sponsored links*), visibly separated by a line and confined to the top edge of the page, or the right hand side of the screen, like the *incipit* and the marginalia in ancient manuscripts.

This is of course even more important at the level of results. PageRank acts alone in classifying relevant answers: No one can buy its ranking. Google's ethical watchword is, variously, a condition or a by-product of PageRank, and indeed, this is their definition of "integrity":

> As we indicate clearly in our results list, certain websites can be associated with a "Sponsored Link" ad. However, Google does not sell positions in these results: in other words, it is not possible

to buy a PageRank value that it higher than the *reality of the Web*. With a Google search, you have a simple, quick, honest and objective solution to finding the highest quality websites, and those whose information answers your needs perfectly.[7]

2. Google applies the same principles to advertising as it does to searches: A less complex algorithm,[8] analogous to PageRank, ranks commercial links, and once again every click is a vote. In other words, the more "we" click on an ad, the higher it appears in the rankings. Even when they pay, advertisers cannot pay to appear first (unlike Overture, for example): We pay only to belong to the "happy few" who appear, and the "quality score" (which is once again nothing but a quantitative score) does the rest.

3. It is ethical that Google's sense of ethics does not influence its search results. Searches should not be influenced because they are the reality of the Web; this is hard ontology. By contrast, Google reserves the right to choose its ads: no pornography, no cigarettes, no beer, although they do allow wine! "We don't try to put our sense of ethics into the search results, but we do when it comes to advertising" (again, the *Playboy* interview).

4. Advertisers finance in the *softest* way possible: When you yourself choose to click on them, it is one cent per click for Google. Advertising is there only to help you, you personally; it loves you, and you love it. Google is *consumer pull* rather than *business push*, where the curiosity of the consumer who does not pay, "your query," counts more than the demand of the company that buys the advertising. In other words, we have gone from a *content-attachment* to an *intent-attachment*.[9] It is your intention, your desire that counts, and the cost of marketing is transformed into profit in direct proportion to how much the keyword reveals this desire.

So we see that advertising and search, kept apart so virtuously, are ultimately one and the same mission. But everything indicates that this mission has been transformed. It has become one of satisfying the *consumer/customer*, and God has lent a helping hand.

> Google's mission is to organize the world's information and make
> it universally accessible and useful. The search results and the
> AdWords ads that appear on Google together contribute to this
> mission.[10]

5. It is the circle itself that is virtuous. Since Google's search results are unbiased, one can trust Google: "People use Google because they trust us." "But people are smart. They can distinguish
pure results," results that are in keeping with the reality of the Web,[11]
such that the earnings of Google come from this goodness itself.
This is what leaves us lost for words. The better it is—and the moral
sense of goodness is from now on confused with the technical sense
of performance—the richer it gets. They were not after money, it
was not the primary goal, but they reached this goal, and this is
proof of their excellence. Just as in *The Protestant Ethic and the
Spirit of Capitalism*, success is proof that they are the chosen ones.

6. The money they make has to then just be well spent, following
the model of charitable good works, for example through a foundation like the one set up by Bill and Melinda Gates, but with Google's
own special touch.

THE DEMOCRACY OF CLICKS AND SOME OF ITS PERVERSIONS

The ranking mechanism is thus a variable that depends more or less
directly on the number of clicks: indirectly, via the number of links,
that is potential clicks, as far as searching is concerned, and directly,
as far as advertising is concerned. Upstream from a generalized free
access, it is this very dependency that Google calls "democracy," as
if the analogy between link or click, and vote, were sufficient proof
of its validity.[12]

The weak spot in this "democracy" is easy to understand. All it
takes is for a link or click to come not from some curious individual, wanting in good faith to find out about or to buy something,
but from someone malevolent, or from a machine programmed by

someone malevolent, producing (or inducing by multiplying the keywords) such a high number of links or clicks that they change the ranking. These kinds of links and click indeed alter this celebrated reality of the Web, of which they are nonetheless an integral part, just as evil is an integral part of the world. The proliferation of false links and invalid clicks, or "trick clicks," is the radical evil of Google/the Web.

The foremost criminal activity is the misappropriation of clicks, and this is true both for ads, and for PageRank:

> What is an invalid click?
> Invalid clicks are clicks generated by illegitimate methods.
> These could be, for example, repeated manual clicks, or clicks
> generated via the intermediary of a robot, an automated tool, or
> any other click misappropriation software.[13]

God, after having created the best mechanism ("The complex and automatic methods used by Google search make any human manipulation of the results almost impossible"), can only monitor ("We monitor closely these kinds of practices to give advertisers better protection against invalid clicks") and punish.

But it is not easy to fathom the intention of a click, especially when perverse behaviors are so wide-ranging. With AdWords one can, for example, click on one's competitors to increase their marketing expenditure or, with AdSense one can click on one's own site franchised by Google to improve one's performance—around 30 percent of clicks could be fraudulent, with the liability resting with the advertiser. The "Rules and Regulations on Invalid Clicks" is a real anthology piece. On the one hand, Google has developed an entire casuist system so it can tell when an advertiser might consider a customer is not real, and thus refuse to pay for the click.[14] On the other hand, it needs to collect a considerable amount of information on the clicker and the click in order to detect whether it is dealing with a fraudulent intention, so what I call "bigbrotherization" becomes a financial necessity. Finally, just as with doping, every time a new system of surveillance is put in place, it is breached, and circumvented by a new type of fraud, requiring a new display of control.[15] "Don't be evil": It is a financial imperative to win the cyber war against all the cheats.

As far as punishment is concerned, the BMW affair was a landmark case. A series of manipulations by BMW Germany and/or whoever "referred" it were alleged to have artificially inflated the company's PageRank. Google blacklisted it, removing it from its index in January 2006. Searches for "BMW" were then directed solely to its official international website. In truth, whether it was able to prove its good faith, or to make some small settlement, its exclusion was short-lived—punishment is in fact a difficult negotiation between the money one earns in demonstrating one's integrity, and the money one earns in compromising one's principles.[16]

The most extreme form of a malicious click is a *Google bomb*. A search can be manipulated in order to obtain a prevalence of certain unexpected links, which is quite easily done since one is at a remove from the query highway, so to speak. Some rather amusing bombs, which have gone unpunished, are more famous than others. So "French military victories" for a long time led to "Did you mean French military defeats?" and the first result for "Miserable failure" since 2003 (and still on July 14, 2006) was the biography of President George W. Bush, translated from Spanish. Today the biography appears even when you simply ask about "miserable" or "failure."[17] To be fair, when one enters "miserable loser" into Yahoo!, two of the first ten results relate to Al Gore.

Finally, there are also unintended sanctions, evils caused by the system without intending to punish, but the outcome of which gives pause for thought. One such example is the sorry tale of 2bigfeet .com. The website of this seller, specializing in large-size shoes, was the "organic" number one, and appeared first through PageRank when you typed the keyword "big feet," as one would "naturally" expect. But when Google did one of its *Google dances*, which is to say one of the regular updates of its algorithm to ward off spam, to take into account new pages, new links, etc., on November 14, 2003—so just before the Christmas shopping period—the website was not only demoted, but quite simply disappeared from the results display. "Google Guys, please listen to what people are saying. . . . Three years' hard work swept away in the space of 24 hours,"[18] as the head of the family might have written, suddenly facing bankruptcy by this systemic effect so devastating for a small business.

The moral of the story was that, in order to reappear on Google, our man had to buy an ad! So we can see how unequal and porous the border is between search (with PageRank in the middle of the page) and advertising (the side ads), and how Google creates a kind of commercial addiction. It is a hard drug (Google or nothing) for the whole "long tail" of the Internet, the gray zone made up of those websites that no one would know about if they did not appear in the right place, one way or another.

One can "optimize" without cheating, one can cheat, and one can also pay: "Eventually people may realize that it's more efficient just to pay to promote their things," Page concludes in the *Playboy* interview. So in France, "*banlieue*" [suburbs] was a keyword bought as an "adword" by Nicolas Sarkozy and the UMP, and in the margins, you could find "*Sécurité, parlons-en*" [Let's talk about security] ("N. Sarkozy and the UMP invite you to discuss plans for 2007"), which gave you access to the UMP website, with a photo of Nicolas, and "Click here to join." On January 14, in the middle of the page the organic result ranked first was "Lilian Thuram lambasts Sarkozy's comments on the *banlieue*," with a link to reuters.fr. By August 2006, the ad had not changed, but the first ranked organic result was "*Copains de banlieue, site pédagogique et ludique . . .*" (Banlieue buddies: Education and play website). You are the Web.

TRANSCENDENCE AND DISCLAIMING RESPONSIBILITY

You are the Web, which is why God has all of the rights but no responsibility.

Deus sive natura of the Web. Even if we can understand why a certain type of responsibility could paralyze the system and prevent an absolute and immanent flow in real time, we are perhaps not really used to a god announcing no guarantees, and not accepting any responsibility for the state of the world:

> We can in no way guarantee that a Google search will not suggest inappropriate or shocking content, and we accept no responsibility for the content of websites . . . including in the results of a Google search.[19]

We are even less used to a god who simultaneously gives himself the right to change his nature and definition, or even to disappear and to leave us stranded. The "Terms of Service" indeed make it clear, as we mentioned at the start of the chapter, that God is authorized "as required, for whatever reason, and without prior notice" to change his laws, to abandon his organization and those he organizes.

To make things absolutely clear, we find at the end of the "Terms of Service" an eloquent and all-inclusive "Disclaimer," in place of the usual "Warranty," and it is even written in capital letters. Just as Google is included in Google, this disclaimer is included within the disclaimer, not even guaranteeing its own legality. I urge you to read it.[20]

It is clear that Google/the Web is giving birth to a new kind of law, adapted to the new objects that make up the "reality of the Web." For now, this law is essentially propitiatory: It opens as widely as possible, by means of the vaguest of formulas, the most immense global umbrella. For the practices corresponding to this "reality of the Web" go "naturally"—we will come back to this[21]—against all existing legislation and regulations, particularly where questions of responsibility and intellectual property are concerned.

We find a similar formulation covering all financial risk resulting from legal problems (including lawsuits) in the report published by Google on June 30, 2004, at the same time as its IPO: "Adverse outcomes in these lawsuits may result in, or even compel, a change

BOX E

Terms and Conditions

Modifying and Terminating our Services

We are constantly changing and improving our Services. We may add or remove functionalities or features and we may suspend or stop a Service altogether.

You can stop using our Services at any time, although we would be sorry to see you go. Google may also stop providing Services to you or add or create new limits to our Services at any time.

We believe that you own your data, and preserving your access to such data is important. If we discontinue a Service, where reasonably possible, we will give you reasonable advance notice and a chance to remove information from that Service.

Our Warranties and Disclaimers

We provide our Services using a commercially reasonable level of skill and care and we hope that you will enjoy using them. But there are certain things that we do not promise about our Services.

OTHER THAN AS EXPRESSLY SET OUT IN THESE TERMS OR ADDITIONAL TERMS, NEITHER GOOGLE NOR ITS SUPPLIERS OR DISTRIBUTORS MAKES ANY SPECIFIC PROMISES ABOUT THE SERVICES. FOR EXAMPLE, WE DO NOT MAKE ANY COMMITMENTS ABOUT THE CONTENT WITHIN THE SERVICES, THE SPECIFIC FUNCTIONS OF THE SERVICES OR THEIR RELIABILITY, AVAILABILITY OR ABILITY TO MEET YOUR NEEDS. WE PROVIDE THE SERVICES "AS IS."

SOME JURISDICTIONS PROVIDE FOR CERTAIN WARRANTIES, LIKE THE IMPLIED WARRANTY OF MERCHANTABILITY, FITNESS FOR A PARTICULAR PURPOSE AND NON-INFRINGEMENT. TO THE EXTENT PERMITTED BY LAW, WE EXCLUDE ALL WARRANTIES.

Liability for our Services

WHEN PERMITTED BY LAW, GOOGLE AND GOOGLE'S SUP-PLIERS AND DISTRIBUTORS WILL NOT BE RESPONSIBLE FOR LOST PROFITS, REVENUES OR DATA, FINANCIAL LOSSES OR INDIRECT, SPECIAL, CONSEQUENTIAL, EXEMPLARY OR PUNI-TIVE DAMAGES.

TO THE EXTENT PERMITTED BY LAW, THE TOTAL LIABIL-ITY OF GOOGLE AND ITS SUPPLIERS AND DISTRIBUTORS FOR ANY CLAIMS UNDER THESE TERMS, INCLUDING FOR ANY IM-PLIED WARRANTIES, IS LIMITED TO THE AMOUNT THAT YOU PAID US TO USE THE SERVICES (OR, IF WE CHOOSE, TO SUP-PLYING YOU WITH THE SERVICES AGAIN).

IN ALL CASES, GOOGLE AND ITS SUPPLIERS AND DISTRIB-UTORS WILL NOT BE LIABLE FOR ANY LOSS OR DAMAGE THAT IS NOT REASONABLY FORESEEABLE.

WE RECOGNISE THAT IN SOME COUNTRIES, YOU MIGHT HAVE LEGAL RIGHTS AS A CONSUMER. IF YOU ARE USING THE SERVICES FOR A PERSONAL PURPOSE, THEN NOTHING IN THESE TERMS OR ANY ADDITIONAL TERMS LIMITS ANY CONSUMERS' LEGAL RIGHTS WHICH MAY NOT BE WAIVED BY CONTRACT.

Business uses of our Services

IF YOU ARE USING OUR SERVICES ON BEHALF OF A BUSI-NESS, THAT BUSINESS ACCEPTS THESE TERMS. IT WILL HOLD HARMLESS AND INDEMNIFY GOOGLE AND ITS AF-FILIATES, OFFICERS, AGENTS AND EMPLOYEES FROM ANY CLAIM, ACTION OR PROCEEDINGS ARISING FROM OR RE-LATED TO THE USE OF THE SERVICES OR VIOLATION OF THESE TERMS, INCLUDING ANY LIABILITY OR EXPENSE ARIS-ING FROM CLAIMS, LOSSES, DAMAGES, JUDGEMENTS, LITI-GATION COSTS AND LEGAL FEES.

About these Terms

WE MAY MODIFY THESE TERMS OR ANY ADDITIONAL TERMS THAT APPLY TO A SERVICE TO, FOR EXAMPLE, RE-

FLECT CHANGES TO THE LAW OR CHANGES TO OUR SER-VICES. YOU SHOULD LOOK AT THE TERMS REGULARLY. WE'LL POST NOTICE OF MODIFICATIONS TO THESE TERMS ON THIS PAGE. WE'LL POST NOTICE OF MODIFIED ADDITIONAL TERMS IN THE APPLICABLE SERVICE. CHANGES WILL NOT APPLY RETROSPECTIVELY AND WILL BECOME EFFECTIVE NO EARLIER THAN FOURTEEN DAYS AFTER THEY ARE POSTED. HOWEVER, CHANGES ADDRESSING NEW FUNCTIONS FOR A SERVICE OR CHANGES MADE FOR LEGAL REASONS WILL BE EFFECTIVE IMMEDIATELY. IF YOU DO NOT AGREE TO THE MODIFIED TERMS FOR A SERVICE, YOU SHOULD DISCON-TINUE YOUR USE OF THAT SERVICE.

If there is any inconsistency between these terms and the additional terms, the additional terms will prevail to the extent of the inconsistency.

These terms govern the relationship between Google and you. They do not create any third party beneficiary rights.

If you do not comply with these terms and we do not take action immediately, this doesn't mean that we are giving up any rights that we may have (such as taking action in the future).

If it turns out that a particular term is not enforceable, this will not affect any other terms.

The courts in some countries will not apply Californian law to some types of disputes. If you reside in one of those coun-tries, then where Californian law is excluded from applying, your country's laws will apply to such disputes related to these terms. Otherwise, you agree that the laws of California, USA, excluding California's choice of law rules, will apply to any dis-putes arising out of or relating to these terms or the Services. Similarly, if the courts in your country will not permit you to consent to the jurisdiction and venue of the courts in Santa Clara County, California, USA, then your local jurisdiction and venue will apply to such disputes related to these terms. Other-

> wise, all claims arising out of or relating to these terms or the services will be litigated exclusively in the federal or state courts of Santa Clara County, California, USA, and you and Google consent to personal jurisdiction in those courts.

in this practice which could result in a loss of revenue for us, which could harm our business. . . . Regardless of the outcome, litigation can have an adverse effect on us because of defense costs, diversion of management resources and other factors."[22] These last three words ("and other factors") are designed to cover the unimaginable, and this last sentence, a kind of golden rule, figures recurrently in all of their monthly reports.

This is the Web: nobody's fault, but somebody's business.

FROM NEW KID ON THE BLOCK TO BIG BROTHER

After the crash of startups in Silicon Valley, after Judge Jackson's ruling against Microsoft and Bill Gates in 2000,[23] Google, with its innocent arrogance, its perpetual inventiveness, its remarkable results as a search engine and then as a company, was quite a nice story, and post 9/11, post-Enron, a nice, clean story. It is no longer the case today, not so much because its principles have changed—even if its success means we see them in a new light—but because Google is in fact very close to being a monopoly, and thus too powerful. Whereas it was the new kid on the block, it is now the embodiment of "Big Brother."

All the World's Data

As usual the reasoning behind this, written into its mission, is frighteningly simple.

The first premise is that Google, in order to become the number-one search engine, has to store all the information in the world, that is, all information from the past and all information from the present, in as close to real time as possible.

The second premise is that everything—everything we know or believe, everything we do, everything that happens, everything we can imagine or hope, everything we feel—can be formatted as information, with a small, big, or enormous loss.

So Google, if it is to conform to its original concept, must be kept virtually informed of everything.

Semantic Web and divine computation

And here we find the decidedly definitional totality of an omniscient God, in the form of a very contemporary ogre called "Big Brother." The one who knows everything at every instant $t1$, including the laws that determine how we get to $t1+1$, is obviously in a position to deduce $t2$. This is pure Leibniz: Divine omniscience is sufficient for predestination. If we know all the predicates of Caesar, we can predict that he will cross the Rubicon. In concrete terms, we are very close to the problem of the semantic Web—*the* next big construction site, with Tim Berners-Lee, the very man who invented the Web, as its demiurge—which is in fact a "logical" Web, that is, it allows for inferences. It no longer works primarily by keywords, but primarily by the tags or metadata that make up a language in the process of becoming optimized (or normalized, to make it interoperable) called RDF, or Resource Description Framework. This language encodes meaning "into the sets of triples that act as subject, verb, and object in an elementary sentence." The Web in this case is no longer "a giant book" (using the academic model of citation), but ultimately "a giant database," and the machine becomes a combination of search engine and reasoning engine.[24] Such a language allows for inferences, even syllogisms, and produces conclusions even in the absence of words *ad locum*. Paul Ford gives an easy to understand example in his article from 2002: "August 2009: How Google beat Amazon and eBay to the semantic Web."[25]

If A is a friend of B, then B is a friend of A.
Jim has a friend named Paul.
Therefore, Paul has a friend named Jim.
Using a markup language called RDF . . . you could put logical
statements like these on the Internet, "spiders" could collect
them, and the statements could be searched, analyzed, and
processed. What makes this different from a regular search is
that the statements can be combined. So if I find a statement on
Jim's website that says "Jim is a friend of Paul" and someone does
a search for Paul's friends, even if Paul's website doesn't have
a mention of Jim on it, we *know* Jim considers himself a friend
of Paul.

Ford explains the problem perfectly: "How does syntax become
semantics? Humans excel at this, but computers are dreadful." This
semantics-syntax interface can obviously be developed for marketing or establishing contacts (putting into contact strangers who
don't know they have what the other is looking for), as Ford pre-
dicted. One can also assume that this would provide a matrix for a
kind of panoptic prediction, and the tools (more effective than the
ordinary Web) for a kind of divine computation.

The vice of incompleteness

We realize how all-encompassing the whole is not only via the
number of pages Google claims to have indexed,[26] but also via the
ever more complex and imaginative platform of tools and services
Google offers to Internet users, who thereby put a considerable
amount of data at Google's disposal, which had until then been
inaccessible. The traditional type of commercial applications aside,
such as Froogle, the online shopping service,[27] every invention is
amazing and instantly becomes indispensable. Among the tools, for
example, are Google Desktop, which allows you to find everything
you have on your computer (and thus indexes it for Google), or
Gmail, which allows you to store almost three gigabytes of email

for free,[28] linked to Google Talk, which allows you to hold a conversation (and thus indexes it for Google). Among their services are Google News, which selects and classifies every fifteen minutes all the news in all the newspapers in the world (and thus indexes it for Google), Blogger, which gives you the means to create and develop your own blog for free (and thus indexes it for Google), or Google Earth, which provides images of everywhere on earth, and thus preserves them for Google.

We can do our best to try to compete with them—the website of the National Geographic Institute, which in France at least provides better images than those of Google Earth, crashed within a few days—but Google will always already have planned an even more inventive expansion or variation: There might soon be a Google Mars! Like a torpedo and a smokescreen, or like an octopus spraying ink, an example of the *mētis* or ruse that the Greeks were fond of, Google makes it announcements instantly because they are always ready to go, it holds back if an announcement makes too many waves, and it is constantly positioning itself in new niches (it apparently offered free Wi-Fi access to everyone living in San Francisco, and like a benevolent boss, has begun with those living in its fiefdom of Mountain View), happy for its left tentacle not to know what its right tentacle is doing. In short, it is always in motion.

We all know that that the two keys to totalization, the two big sites that are under construction for every operator, including Google, are data mining, or the extraction of hidden (implicit, buried) data,[29] and interoperability, that is, the capacity to get several different systems to communicate with one another so they can interact.

It is clear that "everything" and "the most possible of everything" are necessary for computation, and Google, in order to be Google, has to store everything.[30]

But its strength is obviously also its weakness: If you refuse to provide information, you harm its effectiveness. The less you give to it, the less it gives back to us. Incompleteness is a vice, technical and otherwise. Just as a malicious click is a radical evil in the democracy of clicks, a refusal to provide information produces a defect in computational power, which accounts for the strategy of the fait accompli, of cookies, clickthroughs, and scanning of works, with the implicit "silence is consent."[31] In short, you can, we can, blackmail Google. We too can stay away if we choose to. Refusing cookies is one of the immediate ways of staying away: You will not be a clickthrough and an intention, you will not be transformed into data, or not in such a raw way. You can refuse to let the GoogleBot robot crawl your websites, or your emails (so refuse Gmail), or your computers (so refuse Desktop). Refuse to allow them to scan the heritage preserved in your libraries.

The whole question then is knowing what interest or meaning you find in staying away from this Google-world. Are you present in a different and better way elsewhere? And why not also stay away from that world? Who is going against the public good, Google or you? Evil, devil: Who is the devil? After all, tradition has it that the devil is the exception, persevering out of jealousy, and that he should be defeated and unhappy, so you would be the devil in this case. Unless your model of behavior is more organized than the devil's, such as a syndicate of producers setting themselves up against the monopoly of a profiteering boss? This is how Pat Schroeder, president of the Association of American Publishers, sees it (her comments are reported in "Googlephobia"): "A new kind of feudalism . . . the peasants produce the content, Google makes the profit." So that's it: Do you want your share of the profits? Unless, in the final analysis, it is really a question of strategy and of political tactics, and unless politics is the missing dimension of this analysis.[32]

Where Is the Evil?

Google and privacy: Mom's apple pie

The first reproach directed at "Big Brother" is that it is in a position to know everything, including things that are of no concern to it, and that you would prefer to keep secret and private.

The first big outcry is a consequence of Gmail. Gmail offers more and more efficient services, all free, of course.[33] But its financial wizardry meant that one day in April 2004, when a mom sent an apple pie recipe by email to her son, a series of cake recipes and cookbooks appeared at the bottom of his email. This was too relevant to be honest! The email cannot not have been read. What a mom writes to her son should not be read. Google scans your private emails to identify the keywords that generate the ads. The Electronic Privacy Information Center supported their complaint.

The Google Guys replied to *Playboy*, casually wheeling out the heavy artillery. First of all, "Any web mail service will scan your e-mail": We scan it to show it to you, we scan it to ensure that it is not spam, to protect against viruses, or pornography: "All I can say is that we are very up front about it. That's an important principle of ours." So, if only for technical reasons, "you should trust whoever is handling your e-mail." What is more, it is "automated," adds Brin: "No one is looking, so I don't think it's a privacy issue." Didn't you know that a robot is not indiscreet? The most important thing is ultimately the mission: "Our ads aren't distracting, they're helpful." At least, the mission redefined as a help to the customer: "During Gmail tests, people bought lots of things using the ads." "It works well, and it's an example of the way in which we are trying to be good." QED.

The Electronic Frontier Foundation, with Brad Templeton, was satisfied in the end with the proposal to separate Google search from Gmail, since it was the correlation that was a virtual danger. But it is easy to see why the apple pie was only the tip of the iceberg and that, with a growing sense of Googlephobia, it might be hard to tell the difference between reason and paranoia: Every one of us is, through our computer, a database that can be consulted ad infinitum, and which it is a priori possible to put to any use. The "Confidentiality agreement" formulated by Google[34] explains that "connection notebooks" contain information such as your Internet search history, your IP address, the type and language of your web browser, the date and time of connection, one or more cookies allowing your browser to be identified; it stipulates that the personal information you send to other sites via Google can be sent to Google so that the service can be guaranteed or improved, and that Google can determine whether the advertised links have been followed or not—it is all about the *behavior* of the *customer*, for the greater good of the "service" service.[35] This agreement is hardly more reassuring than the disclaimer, and in any case, the disclaimer is in itself sufficient to invalidate it. We go from a one-sided contract to another one-sided contract (in the broader, nonlegalistic sense of the terms "one-sided" and "contract," whether we are talking about a contract of trust or a social contract). Whatever the rules of confidentiality may be, they are subordinate to the supreme ultimate goal of "providing and improving our services." In the same way, you have access to your personal information, you can correct or delete it just by asking, "except . . . when this data is needed for legitimate commercial ends." An entire operation begins to take shape, linked to a marketing ethics that mimics the law, a law that is on the face of it not at all Roman, and very much *common law*. By contrast to the "legitimate" decided in commercial terms, we have the "unreasonable" ("certain requests can be refused in the following instances, as unreasonable requests"), and the "disproportionate" ("provided it does not require a disproportionate effort"). Each of these terms is by definition undefined: even if it aspires to a definition that would itself be legitimate, reasonable, measured, this definition is arbitrary, even discretionary. Indeed, this discretionary element is self-proclaimed in one final proviso clause: "Please note that the present Confidentiality agreement can be changed at any point." We are in a world which only derives its legitimacy from its very operation, basking in the glow of the success of a consensual practice of trust and good faith, based on statements made "beyond reasonable doubt": Swear that you have no intention of assassinating the president of the United States, and sign here . . .

If we realize that interoperability (by which I mean audio and

video mobile phones, barcodes, electronic bracelets and chips im-
planted into things and people—your car, your dog, your child, a
prisoner?—photographic and sound recordings at every point of
the globe at every moment, and I clearly don't really know what I
am talking about with this enumeration) is progressing at the same
time as the archiving and relevance of searches, there is no limit to
information, nor any limit to its use. And if we add to this the fact
that Google is interested in the human genome, that Google Genes,
in which Page is directly involved, is already underway—the fiend-
ish and talented Craig Venter seems to be the driving force behind
the program:[36] "It is the ultimate intersection between technology
and health that will empower millions of individuals." We are closer,
then, to a best of all possible worlds that is really more Orwellian
than Leibnizian.

So no limits, unless we put them in place and respect them.

What were we saying earlier about so long as God is good? Perhaps so long as God is discreet, at any rate.

Google and states: The Patriot Act and the Chinese market

And as long as he does not have a SuperGod above him.

It is all a question of attitude: "Don't be evil," ethical or not, is
an absolute necessity for trust to work. Google will be judged by its
acts either as collaborator or resister, when confronted by the pressure exerted upon it by States to communicate the information it
has, or to twist the information it gives them.

Until now it has been both, but the benefit of doubt doesn't really work here. It is clear that the pressure from states is in fact an
economic pressure, at least as much as it is a juridical and legal
pressure. Even if legal discourse can serve as a camouflage, profit
is an effective means of blackmail. Moreover, what part of this iden-
titarian double bind should Google choose: stop being Google by
agreeing to be evil, or stop being Google by relinquishing all the
world's information? Google behaved well with the Bush administration, and if it also behaved badly, there is no way of knowing

which. But it certainly behaved badly, that is to say no better than the others, with the Chinese government.

Google's first link to 9/11 was the appearance of Google News, which was created in response to the 125 million or so queries a day that were all related not to Britney Spears but to the World Trade Center and to Afghanistan. We should say first of all how much of a game-changer this was: We are no longer allowed not to be informed, and we can always crosscheck the information. Their French site opened with "500 continually updated sources of information," and ended with the warning: "The selection and placement of the articles on this page has been generated automatically by a computer program." Google News is first and foremost an online service that was, of course, free and accessible to anyone on the Internet. It manifestly carries with it rather serious and perverse effects, however. Information, as the work of a journalist, is not simply a mass of news organized by an algorithm, depending on what is available on the Web, and according to the Page-Rank principle: If print journalism is suffering, and it is suffering, it is disastrous for information itself (and thus indirectly for Google News). Objectivity is no more guaranteed because of automation than Gmail's confidentiality is guaranteed because of robotics.

But 9/11 had another kind of repercussion for the media, namely, the Patriot Act. It is worth noting, not without some surprise, that the "USA Patriot Act" was only ever an acronym, including for "USA," a reinterpretation/play on words that replaces "States" with "strength": "Uniting and Strengthening America by Providing Appropriate Tools Required to Intercept and Obstruct Terrorism," an acronymic poetry of kit and fit as the last refuge of the signifier in an information society! The "Patriot Act" was able to compel Google to hand over all the information it had at its disposal, without notifying the people concerned, within the (transgressed?) limits of the Fourth Amendment, which defends private life against the infringement of an "unreasonable search."[37] It was even explicitly designed to bring the 2001 Anti Terrorism Act into the Internet age, and it

opened up the domains of email and Web surfing to their investi-
gations. So that this time it was Google, as the good little brother
confronted by the "very Big Brother" that, as Battelle put it, "stood
alone between your private life and the will of a determined hacker
or a government agent." Indeed, Google did its best to resist the
Bush administration, in contrast to Yahoo!, MSN, and AOL. Google,
by agreement with the Electronic Frontier Foundation, refused to
comply with the Department of Justice, which asked it, in its fight
against pornography (the 1998 Child Online Protection Act), to provide search history data from its website. Google argued that the
summons was "harmful, vague, and intended to harass." Shayana
Kadidal, a lawyer with the Center for Constitutional Rights in New
York City, believed that this could be a "first step before demanding
access to the content of emails." Google thus enhanced its positive
image as a "rebel" and simultaneously recorded a fall of 8.5 percent
in its share value on January 20, 2006.[38] If it did finally give in, the
very content of the Patriot Act means it is impossible to know, since
it is illegal to notify the people concerned. *Very Big Brother* destroys
all trace behind it, and if ever there is a crime, it can only be a perfect crime.

We might add that the Department of Justice is interested in
Google, and even uses it: "It is in the final stages of implementing
the Google search engine." It admires the relevance of its search results, and the speed of its response time: "Google search response
times meet industry standards and are less than 3 seconds." And it is
of course the Agency, the CIA, that is in control: "Response time and
relevancy of search will continue to be monitored by the Agency."
Google is a search engine that offers its technology under license,
for the small percentage of the income that does not come from
advertising, and one could hardly reproach it if the Agency noticed
it was the best.

It was Google's decision, however, not to resist the attraction of
the Chinese market. It complied with the equivalent of an implicit
Patriot Act, but for a foreign country perceived as politically incor-

rect. The headline from *Le Monde* of January 17, 2006, read, "Google the Hypocrite": It respected human rights, but only selectively.

The competition was ferocious. Yahoo! handed over information that led to the journalist Shi Tao's being sentenced to ten years in prison for having sent "secret" documents overseas by email, allowing the account holder of the journalist to be identified, even though it was registered in Hong Kong. It was total war with Microsoft, since the founder of Microsoft-China, M. Lee, lost his job for running "Gu-Ge" (the Chinese homophone means "song of the grain harvest"), and because the lawsuit for unfair competition is underway, not to mention the increasing power of the local search engine Baidu. So Google gave in to the censorship of the Chinese government, which has built a new "Great Wall of China" to block information it does not want. For the sake of comparison, on February 15, 2006, *Libération* published photographs from a search for "Tiananmen Google Images" in France (tanks) and the same search in China (crowds celebrating and lovely parades). Google demonstrated once and for all the incompatibility between its commercial interest and its conception of a democratic imperative, and it opted for commerce with 120 million or so Chinese Internet users. It admits having censored sites that were banned in February 2004, particularly in relation to Tibet, Taiwan, and the protests and their repression in Tiananmen Square. The websites have disappeared so, as Google warns us, users do not need to click on the error messages—as with the Patriot Act, we don't even know that we don't know. Eric Schmidt defended this decision with political double speak: "We promised the Chinese government that we would respect the law, there is no alternative," he said in no uncertain terms, "it is inconceivable that we would disseminate illegal or immoral information."[39] Go to China, and do the least amount of evil possible! The fact remains that the universal objective is no longer credible: We do not have access to the same information via Google in New York as we do in Beijing, and Google agreed to this. On each occasion the law is the singular law of the country that is the source of the query, and not the ethical or democratic law within me, or within the company's culture. We are not dealing with universality, but with economically appropriate universalities.

The most recent episode to date is quite subtle: In the face of the demands of the Chinese government, Google is apparently only too happy to be brought to order by the American government. It has sought, via a number of human rights associations, the support of the American legal system, accepting the outcome of a lawsuit prohibiting it (or any of its American competitors, which is the key point here) from complying with the Chinese demands.

For once, as this banal example demonstrates, being good does not pay. There is a conflict of interest between interest and ethics, and whatever casuistic reasoning "Don't be evil" allows it to develop, playing obedience to a legal law against obedience to an ethical law, it is clear that Google Inc. has come down, and can only come down, on the side of interest.

So we'll get them all, even the people in the trees.

—Eric Schmidt

ON CULTURAL DEMOCRACY

SENSITIVE DATA—OUR BOOKS!

Some data is more sensitive than other data.

When it comes to intimacy and privacy (mom's apple pie recipe) and to inquisition by political or police authorities (the Patriot Act, Tiananmen Square), we can always express the pious wish that a private company such as Google should exercise the right to withhold or withdraw information (thereby contradicting its own status) and should try to help realize this pious wish through appropriate lobbying, boycotting, and competition—in other words, through blackmail and leverage of power.

I would like to explore, however, the Google effect on two other kinds of data that have a more direct impact on culture: our books and our languages. The former caused a scandal, and there is still much to be invented with regard to the latter.

A Brief History: Google Print and Google Book Search

Books are part of "the world's information." However high-tech it is, in any research project whose model and values are "academic," books are an essential source. Even though a book is far from being reducible to information, scanning and indexing books give access to information whose reliability is already guaranteed through an editorial process and/or by a traditional form of recognition, and philological desiderata can thereby be incorporated, at least in part, into the heterogeneous medium of the web.

The pre-Google Larry Page was already working with his professor at Stanford, Terry Winograd, on a "Digital Libraries Project." The Google Larry Page presented his project of mass digitization at a brainstorming session on the idea of a "Final Encyclopaedia" organized by Paul Allen, cofounder of Microsoft, at his home on the San Juan Islands. The University of Michigan (Page's undergraduate university, and the one his father taught at) was the first place this was tested out: Google's special equipment was hidden, like Poe's purloined letter, in plain sight behind the name they gave to the project, the "Michigan Digital Library."[1] After its IPO in October 2004, Google presented its project "Google Print for Publishers" at the Frankfurt Book Fair. Publishers were invited to give their books to Google to digitize (or a "native" digital copy of their books), to index, and to give more or less restricted access to them, depending on the nature of the rights and the contract agreed, by means of keywords.[2] In November 2004, Google announced Google Scholar, a version of their search engine dedicated to indexing scientific and academic literature, whose motto is "Stand on the shoulders of giants." On December 14, with Google Print Library Project, it unveiled its plan to digitize, over the next ten years, 15 million books from the Bodleian library in Oxford, the libraries of Stanford and Harvard, and New York Public Library, at an estimated cost of ten dollars per book. The project was suspended in June 2005 because of copyright problems raised by the Association of American Publishers. It resumed in November 2005 under the name "Google Book Search," which, according to Google, "reflected more exactly the way people were using it," and which emphasized the benefits to the book industry rather than its rivalry with the Gutenberg paradigm. In 2006, "in a moving speech" delivered to the same Association of American Publishers, the president of the University of Michigan, Mary Sue Coleman, explained "why the University has chosen to become our partner" (Google was reporting the speech), underlined "the importance of the digitization of books when confronted with natural catastrophes such as Hurricane Katrina," and added, "We believe in this forever."

The project bore all the hallmarks of Google. It was on an entirely different scale to existing digitizations: Project Gutenberg, launched by Michael Hart in 1971, proposed digitizing 18,000 books online by 2006, according to Wikipedia,[3] the "Million Book Project" at the Carnegie Mellon University was apparently up to 600,000, and Gallica (the digital library of the Bibliothèque Nationale de France) at this point in time gives access to 70,000 volumes as images and 1,200 as text,[4] and this does not include sound and picture files. Google Book Search introduced an exceptionally high quality and rapid but low-cost technology, and it offered a transparent and effective user interface, with a keyword search possible for the entire text (unlike Gallica, which opted originally for image files). It was classic Google also in its policy of the fait accompli, with a critical mass that makes it hard to remain outside, and with a disdain for legal problems when it come to the thorny question of copyright (their style was make or break, but not without some wrangling). It was classic Google finally in its missionary aura: all the information in the world for everyone, and on to a better world.

Resistances

There was from the outset a synergy between three types of resistance:

1. An emotional reaction from Europe, initiated by the president of the Bibliothèque Nationale de France (Jean-Noël Jeanneney, January 2005, in a commentary in *Le Monde*, and then in his book *Quand Google défie l'Europe* [When Google Challenges Europe], April 2005). This culminated in the creation of an alternative, the

European Digital Library, linked to the TEL (The European Library) program, which gave access to the catalogue and digitized content of eight national libraries (rising to forty-four when complete), which all francophone libraries belong to, and which was taken up by the project call launched by the European Commission (i2010 Digital Libraries). The "White Paper" of the European Digital Library highlighted as the most interesting initiative the Börsenverein (the German equivalent of the Cercle de la Librairie [Book Retailers Network]), with its project Volltextsuche Online (Full Text Online Search), presented in May 2005, which brings together the local (local platforms for data management) and the global (multiaccessibility of data via the greatest possible number of search engines), the private (German publishers and booksellers), and the public (libraries), with horizontal and vertical integration of all of the core trades that have anything to do with books.[5]

2. An outcry from publishers, authors, and copyright holders that started in the United States but spread around the world, with ongoing court cases in a number of countries (particularly Agence France Presse and La Martinière/Le Seuil in France).

3. Finally, a competition, or a "coopetition," to borrow one of Google's terms, among the different parties, beginning with the "Open Content Alliance" formed in October 2005 as an initiative of the "Internet Archive"—the brilliant Brewster-Kahle[6]—and linked at first to Yahoo!, while for its part the British Library signed an agreement with Microsoft, in response to the Library of Congress confirming its plan to create a "World Digital Library" financed by Google.[7]

A can of worms with good intentions, to which Google Inc. has now accustomed us.

The Troublesome Problem of Rights
Justifying the fait accompli

The thorniest question is the question of rights, particularly since the rules and regulations differ from one country to the next.[8] For works that are part of a cultural heritage and that are in the public domain, the question does not arise. For works that are under copyright, Google justifies digitizing them, under the aegis of its mission, in the following way:

1. A policy of the fait accompli is a necessity: It is an *Alexandrian project*, a Herculean mission, and if we had to ask the permission of all the rights holders, the project would simply become impossible, both in terms of time and cost.

2. When works are under copyright, Google does not give access to their digitized copy, but gives access only to bibliographic information about the work and, through a keyword search, to "snippets" (the definition of which remains vague) related to these keywords; when these keywords are recurrent terms in the book, it gives access to three snippets, and no more than three.

3. Following a procedure "inspired" by the Digital Millennium Copyright Act, Google takes note of copyright infringement complaints ("Copy out the following sentence: 'I believe in good faith that the use of the material in the manner complained of is not authorized by the copyright owner, its agent, or the law' . . . Your signature."), even if any complaint can itself be contested by a contradictory declaration coming from the incriminated site.

The angelic Google doesn't understand "why such a useful tool is so *controversial.*"[9] There should be something for everyone there, not only for users who obtain quality information but also for publishers and authors (and sometimes now even for local bookstores), who sell more thanks to increased visibility and free advertising.

4. Copyright holders (in particular the American Association of Publishers and the Authors Guild) have taken it upon themselves to explain to Google that it has a digital copy of something that does not belong to it, that it has neither bought nor asked for. It turns copyright law on its head, reverses the burden of proof by proposing an opt-out (you have to ask Google to get out) instead of an opt-in (Google should ask you to join). We are back once again, as with cookies, to the fait accompli of silence as consent.[10]

5. Assuming copyright infringement is proven, Google comes back with another argument, that of fair use, linked to common law and the first amendment.[11] Fair use is an "equitable rule of reason," which authorizes noncommercial use for educational purposes, "such as criticism, comment, news reporting, teaching, scholarship or research."[12] The arguments in favor of Google on the grounds of fair use are the following: The whole copy is not made available (just "snippets"), it is not used for direct commercial ends (even if it does generate profits through the additional information and ads), and it does not harm any commercialization carried out by the copyright holders. Quite the opposite, in fact, since it is an incidental stage in the creation of a new object with considerable added social value, that is, indexation. The plaintiffs, on the other hand, argue against this interpretation of fair use by saying that Google is facilitating fraud and unauthorized usage, and that there is a commercial detriment in being deprived of the opportunity to take part in the creation of databases that have been your initiative and under your control.

Unfair use and the fallout from the Google/Michigan affair

What is clear as concerns the legal grounds of fair use is that a book is considered to have the potential for added value: its transformation into information. From my perspective as a philosopher, it is not copyright which is turned on its head, it is the notion of culture itself,[13] and that should be the starting point for any discussion about what a cultural Web means, and how digital libraries can contribute to it.

I would like to argue that the change of medium that digitization represents, even though it is chronologically posterior, is not in and of itself posterior, or superior. On the contrary, it is anterior to new uses and new cultural practices. Indeed, the "documentary" Web represents one stage in the evolution of the cultural Web that is, in the language of the *attorney*, a socially useful transformation.

That said, I would like now to reflect at greater length on the question of rights.

First of all, as concerns Google's attitude, it is *reasonable* that *fair use* in its far-reaching inventiveness applies to everyone. Google cannot at the same time "authorize" itself and "prohibit." This is, however, what it did with the University of Michigan, even if the University, eternally in love, did not complain. There is a cultural "fair use" which adds something to the digital copy created by Google, and thus a fair use by Google that Google is wrong, legally and morally, to prohibit (we are, just as in Rawls's theory of "Justice as Fairness," immediately immersed in a moralization that is untranslatable in French). As I write this, in early August 2006, all of the agreements between Google and its different partners are secret, except for one, the first one signed with the University of Michigan, and which we can find on its website. It stipulates basically that the utilization and dissemination of the digital copy are subject to Google's discretion, whereas Google for its part is subject to nothing and reserves the right to index the whole text, as well as to use the complete image.

4.4.1. . . . U of M shall restrict access to the U of M Digital Copy to those persons having a need to access such materials and shall also cooperate in good faith with Google to mutually develop methods and systems for ensuring that substantial portions of the U of M Digital Copy are not downloaded from the services offered on U of M's website or otherwise disseminated to the public at large.

4.4.2. . . . U of M shall have the right to use the U of M Digital Copy, in whole or in part at U of M's sole discretion, as part of services offered in cooperation with partner research libraries such as the institutions in the Digital Library Federation. Before making any such distribution, U of M shall enter into a written agreement with the partner research library and shall provide a copy of such agreement to Google, which agreement shall: (a) contain limitations on the partner research library's use of the materials that correspond to and are at least as restrictive as the limitations placed on the U of M's use of the U of M's Digital Copy in section 4.4.1.

4.5.1. Google may use the Google Digital Copy, in whole or part at Google's sole discretion.

The reason for this, the University apologizes, is that it would have taken us 1,600 years and cost us hundreds of millions of dollars to convert this data ourselves. We have chosen first and foremost to carry out our mission to preserve our cultural heritage, and we accept limiting ourselves to a marginal use of advanced research.

There is no excuse for Google, though. It prohibits any synthesis or synergy between culture and information, or between the different formats of the book, and its many uses. Instead of simply making it freely available, it protects its own use of it, through its own indexing and classifying, and prohibits any other use. Google is neither *fair* nor reasonable; indeed, it is unreasonable that Google should benefit from a *fairness* it refuses others.

Copyright/copyleft: *In the same direction as the Web?*

I might add, more generally, that it seems to me quite difficult not to revisit the whole question of *copyright* as a more or less long-term question. If Google is "wrong" selectively to retain exclusive rights, it is more broadly "right" to advocate free online open access. There are obvious things that are difficult to say when one is an author, when one edits a collection, or is part of a larger national or European editorial team, and yet that are impossible not to say.

In fact, even when one is an author or publisher, one runs up against the perverse effects of protection, in particular in relation to translation. When a work enters into the public domain seventy years after the death of its author, it is not however necessarily the case for the translation of this work in a given language. So not only do you have to pay to quote the French translation of Pessõa, for example, but you are not allowed to propose any other translation, more or otherwise exact and appropriate to the context of what you are saying. The untranslatable is what one never stops (not) translating,[14] but the rules and regulations of rights blocks this movement, which is indispensable for criticism and for thought. There is an urgent need to invent a different set of rules and regulations.

A few good sense remarks first of all on the sense or direction of the Web, as one says of the direction of fur, for example. These remarks could be open to the same reproach of "naturalization" or "organicity" for which I have critiqued Google's idea of the "reality of the Web," if they did not expressly introduce an extrinsic dimension, which is the political dimension.

1. The Web is obviously worldwide, so Europe's Web function can be only strategic or tactical, and linked to a politics.

2. The Web is obviously free, both in terms of free content (which is obviously not without considerable problems), and free access to this content.

3. The notions of *open source* ("By open source we mean any communication, interconnection or exchange protocol, and every format of interoperable data, whose technical specifications are public and with no restriction of access or implementation"[15]) and of interoperability ("the fact that several systems, whether they are identical or radically different, can communicate without ambiguity and operate together") obviously go in the same direction as the Web.

4. *Copyleft*, a term invented by Don Hopkins ("Copyleft, all rights reversed!") and developed by Richard Stallman—both a leftwing copy as well as a copy that is left alone—unlike copyright obviously goes in the same direction as the Web. *Copyleft* is all the more effective in that it uses *copyright* to cancel out its effects, the contract of use taking the form of a free license (GNU, or General Public License, which was first used on free software such as Unix or Linux), implying by extension the respect of this freedom by the users.

5. Restrictions on consultation (specialized terminals, authorized establishments, on site consultation, types of use and of user, and so on), including those of *fair use*, and of EU law, obviously go in the opposite direction to the Web.[16]

6. The best of all Webs in the best of all possible worlds (but how can we say this without irony?) would obviously contain all books, in all languages, freely accessible for all, everywhere in the world.

7. The Web is obviously first and foremost a constantly expanding digital warehouse, and the various ways of organizing, structuring, and using its contents are also constantly differentiated and constantly expanding.

8. The Web is what we will make of it. But just who is this "we"?

The astonishing contortions of *copyright* are quite regressive, even if they are strategically necessary at a certain point in time, the time of transition and mutation in which we currently find ourselves. It is clear that they run counter to what is commonly referred to as the new paradigm (as François Stasse notes, they are regressing even further back than the Gutenberg paradigm, when the principle was one of freedom of access to the printed work, and restricting access was only an exception). By definition, one cannot partition off a network, and there is no longer such a thing as a rarity, except if one thinks in terms of added value for cyber-entrepreneurs. In short, "it becomes very difficult to justify property rights such as they were established at the beginning of industrial capitalism."[17]

The question of *copyright* is closely linked to that of the *trademark*, and here again, Google/the Internet has already won. The collusion between technical reasons linked to the functioning of the Web, and ideological reasons linked, to put it simply, to the correctness of alter-globalization principles, has become unavoidable. As far as the technical aspect is concerned, its symbol is the GEICO/ Google court case, which the insurance company GEICO lost. If you click on "GEICO" it takes you to other rival sites, which can appear in the center of the page before GEICO. Google's response is the following: "We carefully weigh up two objectives: the protection of the trademark right and making available to our users information that is as complete and relevant as possible." The judgment passed down stipulated that "GEICO has not proven that the use of the trademark name alone as a search term or keyword caused the confusion."[18] In short, it would not be Google's fault if GEICO is not the best insurance company and if people know it ("You are the Web"). Basically, brand names become generic terms through keyword searches. This is where we come back, precisely, to the alter-globalist demands for free sharing when the stakes are very high, by analogy with open sourcing and interoperability: health and medicine ("generic" brands), genomes (which cannot be patented), ecology and the perverse protection GM crops enjoy (is this a case of patents preventing the planet from being a better place to live?), with no indication of where this list might end.

What is still unclear is who pays for the rules and regulations governing the Internet (which themselves also have to be defined, so would these involve, for example, rules surrounding spam and pornography, or against the dissemination of false information or incitement to hate?), and how to remunerate "authors" as well as the chain of all those involved in the book trade. All of this is being made up as it goes along. As far as books are concerned, there are several interconnected considerations, all hypothetical since we still do not have enough distance, and because we are a long way from any kind of stability (digital paper, e-books, the Internet itself are, for the most part, still to come):

1. It is by no means certain that access to digital works is disadvantageous to "print media." It is not the same object and does not involve the same use, the same temporality, or the same pleasure.[19]

2. One might imagine, instead of a watertight security system strengthening the legislation (which, it has to be said, is considered excessively authoritarian in France),[20] a fixed sum of money charged at source, for example on each computer or printer sold, similar to the charge introduced in France for photocopying, with an appropriately equitable and well managed redistribution of funds.

3. One can consider public/private partnerships as self-evident, as well as horizontal and vertical synergies, whether with search engines, software, material, technologies, or content, like the synergies beginning to emerge with the "Quaero" program, which brings together European industrial businesses (Deutsche Telekom, France Télécom, and Thomson), technology companies (Bertin Technologies, Exalead, Jouve, LTU, and Vecsys), research institutes (the INRA, the CNRS, Clips/Mag, RWTH-Aachen, and the University of Karlsruhe), as well as content providers (including the BnF, the INA, and Studio Hamburg).

4. One can even not be offended by the relationship between culture, documentation, and information/advertising, and with public services (universities, libraries) as well as public television channels allowing for certain kinds of well-monitored paying advertisements (less intrusive and more relevant than on television—precisely the kind of ad one finds on Google). Let Quaero (the program) or Exalead (the search engine) earn as much money as Google if they can, as long as they can provide access for everyone to good and inventive ways of structuring works and knowledge.[21]

5. However one looks at it, every "core trade," as the White Paper calls them, should probably refocus on the things it does well. Libraries should more than ever "librarize" and "e-librarize," editors should edit and "e-edit," with each of these core verbs requiring a redefinition.

A European digital library

It is very difficult to know how far back to stand to have the least false perspective possible on what is happening, and which is evolving every day. What motivates a library to refuse to allow Google to digitize its books? What motivates the Bibliothèque Nationale de France to do this, unlike the Library of Congress?

Some advantages and disadvantages are obvious, while others are a matter of negotiation.

As far as the cost is concerned, Google takes care of digitization.

It is a priori stupid, both from an economic and global point of view and from a given library's point of view, to invest in duplications when there is so much to be done.

As for technology, there are differences of opinion. Some talk of new technology that is not only superfast, but also ultrarespectful, so that even Harvard agrees to allow Google to digitize its incunabula, while others talk of irresponsibility, and lack of quality in the results. It is a priori reasonable to adopt a policy that consists of digitizing the maximum number of non-rare works possible.

In terms of copyright, one needs to make a distinction between works in the public domain and works under copyright. It is a priori reasonable to digitize the maximum number of works possible in the public domain, which pose no problem, just as it is reasonable to recommend to publishers that they keep a meticulous original digital copy. It is also reasonable to include in the rules and regulations the distinction François Stasse proposed between not two but three domains, the third being made up of "orphan works" of which we do not know the copyright holders, and of that whole "gray zone" of works that are chronologically still under copyright, but commercially not available, which could provisionally be considered as belonging to the public domain. Unless we breathe new life into this taxonomy by proposing ways out of the gray zone in case of works that are rediscovered and could potentially generate profits, like Vermeer, whose brilliance as a painter was only recognized several centuries after his death. It is worth pointing out that Google nowadays boasts of compensating libraries for the cost of any potential lawsuit.

If the problems of cost, technology, and copyright are all resolved, what is holding things up?

The answer is the question of ownership of the digital copy, and the use Google conceded contractually to the library. Nothing is possible if it is a "Michigan" type contract, but if one takes a more forceful position, defended and supported by a battalion of interlocutors that are significant, symbolically and practically speaking (a majority of national libraries of European universities and museums, but not just European), and one has no hesitation playing the competition card (the White Paper talks of "opportunistic alliances with search engines aimed at specific operations"), then one is perhaps in a position to negotiate digitization with full and free use of the copy, including the possibility of having access to it through rival search engines.

If this were the case, all the more reason to proceed on the basis of the particular skills of this battalion of interlocutors.

To move from a digital warehouse to a usable selection, one can obviously envisage several different forms of mediation. PageRank is an incomparable (and unstoppable) organization whose doxic-American limits we commented on earlier. These limits certainly create a significant and troubling bias for works and for "culture" as such, and Jean-Noël Jeanneney is right to draw attention to Google's "gondola end,"[22] however much it claims to be the "reality of the Web," which will never correspond to the structure or structuring of knowledge that a library, a university, a museum, a department of national education, or of the culture of a nation-state, or a commission of the European Union would be entitled to want, not only for its own people but for everyone.

A partial solution would be to accept Google's offer of digitization (or the offer of a private company like Google), provided one can retain free use of the digital copy. One would then propose, by means of different types of (more "semantic") indexation and other ways of structuring the data, very different added value for the digitized collection. Google would thus be both invested from the inside, enriched by content which seems significant to "us"—we are the Web, we are part of one and the same world—and used from the outside in order to help give access to other digital worlds to which we "all" lay claim as well. A virtual library made up of books and not only of information, the best editions presented and critiqued using the necessary apparatus, an observatory of websites, an observatory of translations, the means through which to find one's way among the different strata of opinions: We have to take a chance on exploiting our particular skills in order to structure information and make people think.[23] Quality, using other algorithms than PageRank, will no longer be an emergent property of quantity, but a matter of history, expertise, diversity, cultures, and culture.

This leaves the question of content: Should we think in terms of "European content," or could the added value of the different ways of structuring itself be considered as content? For my part, and like many philosophers (Kantian-Derridean, let us say), I am fearful of the idea of a European identity that has its point of reference in an essence of Europe, since this essence can only be formed on the basis of commonplace notions, such as a constitutive "melting pot," "democracies and public freedoms," and even "cultural heritage," which to me contradict the very idea of universality Europe is supposed to be promoting.[24] We assume that this set of values comes out of the Enlightenment, but in my view, the universality of the Enlightenment is precisely a formal universality, which is not connected to any particular content, but to the possible universalization of this content, with a center as empty as Kantian moral law. A European identity that is positively conceived runs the risk of being a *doxa* as frightening as a democracy of clicks, or an "ethical" marketing— as Jean Beaufret said, "a destroyer is still first and foremost a torpedo boat" [*un contre-torpilleur est d'abord et avant-tout un torpilleur*]. The United States likes to think of itself as the original "melting pot," and Google is constantly promoting "democracy": Nothing is as easily shared, even if only in the form of a homonym, as good identities in the form of good grades.

The notion of "cultural heritage," which seems to be self-evident, is particularly fraught with paradoxes: It implies a legacy and preservation of an identity, rather than dissemination and plural invention. Culture, though, like a language, is caught between the two, in a kind of self-otherness.[25]

It is of course important for Europe to make available to the rest of the world something like a European cultural heritage—which

I would prefer to think of, using UNESCO's terminology, as a part of the cultural heritage of humanity—and it is indeed the task of a European library to preserve this heritage, by which I mean works written by "Europeans" (would these be natives of Europe, or those living in Europe?) in the different languages of Europe (would one include those written in the Spanish and Portuguese of Latin America, in the English of the United States, of Asia, and of South Africa, in the French of Africa, of the Caribbean, and of Canada? Or in Sanskrit, Greek, Latin, as well as Hebrew or Arabic, as languages of intellectual trade?), with their translations, their criticisms, their interpretations, and their traditions (would one include Parmenides and Marx in Russian and Chinese, for example?). It is an excellent strategy to begin with what seems essential to us for an understanding of this open Europe, with its problematic identity, since this is not to be found (or is hard to find) on the Internet, and will not be found unless we decide to put it there, especially given how fragile the medium is for this currently, at least in terms of audiovisual heritage. One of the excellent works in progress of the Bibliothèque Nationale de France and of the Bibliothèque Numérique de l'Union Européenne is thus the digitization of the "magazines and newspapers informing debates and opinions (from *Mercure de France* to *Figaro* to *L'Humanité*)," which enables us to understanding how "public opinion" is formed, and thereby to put into perspective the *doxa* of Google as the "reality of the Web."

On the other hand, it would be both contradictory and counterproductive for a "European" library, as well as search engine, to stop at a "European" definition of the data. This data is not intended to be limited to Europe, but is harvested in a global flow, in space and in time. As Umberto Eco says, "the language of Europe is translation," and we have to affirm that European data is multicultural (and not just linked to the cultures of Europe), as well as multilingual (and not just linked to the languages of Europe). Let us imagine it as the last avatar of European expansionism. It is unfortunately by no means certain that this is the most plausible interpretation of the first text "establishing a community program several times a year—named '*eContentplus*'—that aims to make European digital content more accessible, easier to use and easier to exploit" (the Official Journal of the EU, decision of March 9, 2005). It is designed to pave the way for a "structured framework of high-quality digital content in Europe—the European space for digital content . . ." (I appreciate the word "structured" here), and to encourage the "creation of large user groups tasked with analyzing and testing out models of prenormalization and specifications *with a view to integrating the multicultural and multilingual aspects of Europe within the process of defining worldwide norms* relating to the digital content studied" (my emphasis). The directives in French, as they are published and thus to be taken as authoritative, lead one at any rate to fear the worst for multilingualism and multiculturalism. We read in the first item in French: "The evolution of the information society and *the appearance of wide bands* are going to influence the lives of all EU citizens" [*"L'évolution de la société de l'information et l'apparition des larges bandes vont influencer la vie de tous les citoyens de l'U.E."*].[26] If you say so . . .

Promoting "culture" as European know-how simply means, in my view, starting out from the past, from specific works that are both historically and timelessly situated, and from differences of languages, rather than starting out from the present as a flow from quantifiable *doxai* and from "everything-in-English." The alternative to Google involves exploring everything Google has to put aside: the singular, style, the work of art, the plurality of language and of cultures as such. Such data constitutes structured collections, and many of these have yet to be invented, according to varied ways of structuring knowledge, which allow for other kinds of searches and results than PageRank. We need to propose another kind of hierarchy that is not "organic," generated by the system. In particular, rank will not depend (primarily) on the number of links and clicks, even weighted. The relevance of an answer will not depend (primarily) on the intention of the user whom his or her clickstream identifies behaviorally as a "consumer," but rather on a plurality of "structurers," that is, experts and masters, who can overlap with the categories of producers, curators, and/or users, with all the dangers that such mastery implies. Alter-globalization as deglobalization.

So what is to be gained by having a European library, when confronted by a project such as Google Book Search, is not a European identity, but on the one hand a guarantee (which begins with a description) of the reliability of the data, and on the other hand alternative hierarchies to PageRank, with everything having a worldwide reach and authority. Nothing after all prevents us thinking here that "Europe" has within its reach one of the least toxic contemporary avatars of its most ancient role.

We need in effect to look at the problem the other way round, and as in judo, use a kind of sweeping hip throw, borrowing the ancient techniques of rhetoric and of the pancratium that have been revived by the martial arts: What is it that Google cannot do, or is not doing, and that "we" want at all costs? What is it in Google that could facilitate what "we" want? We have to begin at the point Page reached when he stated that a perfect search engine is "a reference librarian with complete mastery of the entire corpus of human knowledge,"[27] and made it immediately clear, borrowing the alternative proposed by Jean-Michel Salaün, that a well-controlled library on a worldwide scale should not privilege one dominant culture but rather give access to minority cultures and little-known texts.

A "European" Search Engine

When Jacques Chirac announced the launch on April 26, 2005, at the council of French and German ministers of a European search engine to rival Google, Quaero ("to search," in Latin), and announced it again on April 25, 2006, the world rightly wondered what sense it made to attach the adjective "European" to a search engine. The answer, like the project, comes in several stages.

It was first of all a strategic alternative to Google (and to the "big four," all American). "Search engines on the Internet are the doors giving access to digital knowledge and to electronic trade. We have to take up the global challenge of the American giants Google and Yahoo!" (Jacques Chirac, "Voeux aux forces vives" [New Year's Address to the Nation], January 5, 2006). It is our turn to say "Our mission": a mission to balance political power, capable of confronting a "don't be evil" that is not respected. We need to maintain a "European" portal as another means to access the same content, in opposition to the "American" one, and to safeguard this access to data, which could be concealed, partially or wholly, by Google, just as Galileo was created in opposition to GPS. The link between the two was made by Jean-Luc Moullet, director of the Galileo project and vice president of software solutions at Thomson, in his presentation to Agence France-Presse in January 2006.

GPS, the Global Positioning System, is run by the US Department of Defense. Twenty-four satellites allow each and every one of us to locate our position by triangulation. All that is needed is to buy a machine for a few hundred dollars that synchronizes the signals. A military code gives the position to within a meter and is changed every ten seconds. A civilian code gives a position to within one hundred meters. The key point is that if the US Department of Defense wanted to make one zone clearer or another one more obscure, it could. So during the Iraq war "they" made the theater of operations clearer for aviation, so that at a stroke, Iraq was no longer covered. The International Civil Aviation Organization (ICAO) depends on GPS. Any free infrastructure is suspect, and even more so if it becomes indispensable, to the point where we become addicted to it, whence the strategic importance of Galileo. A European search engine would thus be designed to fulfill the same role as an alternative, except that the alternative already exists, is even multiply present through international competition, and to complicate the picture the Internet, which was originally a Defense Department Project, is still dependent on what we might call "American-global" rules and regulations.[28]

BOX F

The Digital Airbus!

This is how Jean-Luc Moullet, head of projects and vice president of software solutions at Thomson, presented Galileo and Quaero to the Agence France-Presse in January 2006:

The two names Galileo and Quaero do not perhaps mean much to you, yet they are both two ambitious European projects. Galileo is the codename used to refer to the European system of radio navigation and global satellite positioning of the future. This is a new system that will compete with the present GPS, and that will give a more precise location, to within a metre, as well as open up new areas of application in navigational and positioning technology.

Additionally, Galileo will offer five main services as opposed to the two offered by GPS: one will be available free of charge and intended for the general public (drivers, motorcyclists, mobile phone users . . .), another will be aimed at airlines, rail travel and shipping transport. The introduction of Galileo will definitively break the monopoly held by GPS.

The first satellite (Giove-A) to be used by the Galileo system was successfully put into orbit today. The second test launch (of Giove-B) will take place in the spring of 2006. If everything goes according to plan, the system made up of 30 satellites should be fully operational by 2010.

The second project, named Quaero ("to search" in Latin) is more connected to the Internet, since its aim is to establish a fast, high-performance European search engine to compete with the American Google, which at the moment reigns supreme on the Web.

Several European initiatives are linked to this project (it

is worth noting in particular the involvement of Thomson, France Télécom and Deutsche Telekom), which should create a search engine that has a greater emphasis on multimedia. Searches will thus include audio, photo or video documents, which would be well indexed, and the search will be as much visual as textual.

The first details of the search engine will be unveiled in January, but we already know that it will be based on technologies of transcription, indexing and automatic translation of multilingual audiovisual documents, as well as on the recognition and indexing of images. The project is ambitious, and it is already being referred to as the "Digital Airbus." The search engine should be fully operational by Summer 2006. Finally, we should mention that Asia is also developing its own search engine thanks to the help of several universities and businesses such as Matsushita, Hitachi, NEC and Fujitsu."[1]

NOTE

1. [Quaero ceased to exist at the end of 2013. As of December 2015 the Galileo system had twelve of thirty satellites in orbit. It planned to offer early operational capability by 2016 and then reach full operational capability with all thirty satellites by 2020. —Trans.]

What is at stake politically is thus immediately inflected in economic and technological terms: "We are going to launch Quaero, a European search engine, with the support of the Agence de l'Innovation Industrielle [Industrial Innovation Agency]. Our aim is to create a new generation of search engines: a truly multimedia search engine integrating sound and image, as well as text" (Jacques Chirac, New Year's Address to the Nation, January 5, 2006). The emphasis of this Franco-German initiative was on multimedia, interoperability (between the different service providers), and convergence (between the different modes of access, such as telephone, television, and Internet). The agency apparently provided 90 billion euros, the largest-ever development aid budget—"a flagrant case of misguided and useless nationalism," American commentators said. Quaero—and the name of the program is rather unfortunate, even if it is not a brand but a project, since quaero.com belongs to an American company which advertises itself as "accelerating marketing performance"!—is linked to Exalead (François Bourdoncle, the driving force behind it, pronounces it "lead" as in "leader"),[29] the search engine proper. It has 4 million Web pages, will soon have 8, perhaps even 12 or 16, and its strategy is to position itself as a challenger to Google and Microsoft, as a third robber baron targeting first businesses, and then everyone (but "your average Joe considers that it is a bit *much*," says Bourdoncle), more or less expensive depending on the product, with a more assistive way of searching ("ultimately more feminine," he says again).

In short, it is clear this is not a different approach to searching worldwide, but for the time being a directly entrepreneurial vision, which will perhaps help marginalize PageRank a little—so more like traditional competition than a new concept altogether.

OUR LANGUAGES!

The Information Technology Idiom

The information technology idiom, not the one used by computer programmers, but that of the users that we are, is a double idiom.

There is first of all a strange idiom used to describe our current practice. This description is made up of concrete images, and immediate metaphors, taken from everyday life and from nature, so the language of technology is a highly initiatory, almost delirious added value. One has to share an appetite for the fabulous to understand the meaning of the Web, spiders, worms, or the meaning of to crawl or to browse. The realm of the virtual is somewhere between the most abstract or fantastic, and the most concrete or empirical, following the formula of fairytales or science fiction, which bind us to the here and now with all the force of everyday detail, to then send us off without warning to another virtual world. One could start with the word "bit" (morsel, piece, bite) as a name for the new object. It is something or nothing, impulse or no impulse, which has now taken the place of the thing or of substance, in a reinterpretation of ontology and semantics. A schoolboy feverishness means that even the great inventors (such as Roland Moreno) circulate inestimably silly jokes or games, so silly that they could have come from Lewis Carroll. A new kind of universalism resets culture, ignoring its own status as an accomplished cultural product, with no apparent depth or history, so that common sense often merges with a sense of humor. Here French, in its resistance to empirical snobbery, is more German than ever: When you translate the metaphors that make up the information technology lexicon, you get the slightly risqué but oh so trendy gibberish (the sort you find at every step when you "translate this page"), such as for example, *"un dessus de bureau dans une salle à vivre"* [literally: "a top of desk in a room for living"], that is to say, "a desktop in a living room."

Then there is the idiom we are forced to use by information technology, from the overlap between natural language and the language of interface. In order to be understood by the computer, we have to speak and think in keywords, tags, go through the narrow portal of the program. Processing information on the computer forces natural language to become uniquely parsimonious and conformist, and we experience this every time we fill out an online or evaluation form. It is a sport that consumes a vast amount of individual time, with the aim of formatting this time to adapt it to the time of the computer. In any event, never will there have been an organization with such often incompetent management and governance, which, under the pretense of equity and objectivity, has been so intrusive.

Google's Languages: Flavors and a Single Main Course

The idiomatic standardization of languages and forms of thought constitutes one of the principal frameworks of "Globish,"[30] or Global English, and determines how the categories are established. However many languages are taken into account, the natural language of the Information Technology idiom is essentially Anglo-American. So whenever the omnipresent multilingual or translation services are offered by Google, they all pivot around "Globish." Wherever you may be, Google starts from where you are and takes it into account. It speaks your language, or something that resembles your language: "With so many of our loyal users around the world, it only seems fair to offer our search services in a variety of linguistic flavors."[31] *Loyal, fair, flavors,* 104 of them to date, all *made in the USA* . . .

Google has gone to remarkable lengths, and we would be wrong to sulk. My reticence, which will perhaps be clear by now, has to do with the idea of what a language is, and to which the word *flavor* bears witness. A language is a flavor, a spice, a familiar taste, to be added to the single main course that is Anglo-American. In this respect, there is nothing original about Google; it is merely part of what makes up a worldwide *doxa*. The only interest of a multilingualism conceived and practiced in this way is a marketing one: The consumer is shown that the product is made for him or her. It thus becomes a single language, already a long way from the natural language that is the English of writers and literary works, a language in folk costume.[32]

This conception of a single language has, *mutatis mutandis*, a long and distinguished history. Anglo-American is, like Koine Greek, or Latin, or to a lesser extent French, a language of empire. It is the language of American diplomacy, economics, and technology, which has de facto become the language of international communication, but it also justifies itself philosophically: It is necessary, and sufficient, to think that languages are the clothes worn by a concept, and that the clothes are of little importance. What counts is the concept, not the word—Aristotle is my colleague at Oxford. Here we also find the Plato of the *Cratylus*, for whom a tool is good independently of the matter that forms it once it has been adapted, or in a more mathematical sense, Leibniz and his notion of a universal characteristic. We are even within the tradition of the Enlightenment project: "Thus, before the end of the eighteenth century, a philosopher who would like to educate himself thoroughly concerning the discoveries of his predecessors will be required to burden his memory with seven or eight different languages. And after having consumed the most precious time of his life in learning them, he will die before beginning to educate himself. The use of the Latin language, which we have shown to be ridiculous in matters of taste, is of the greatest service in works of philosophy, whose merit is entirely determined by clarity and precision, and which urgently require a universal and conventional language."[33] Google is indeed in fine philosophical company, which leads one to think of Anglo-American as a plausible ersatz of a universal language, especially since it already exists.

I would like to make a plea, however, for an entirely different conception of the difference between languages and of multilingualism.[34] We need to start with Humboldt's affirmation that "language only appears in reality as a multiplicity."[35] Such that, as he goes on to say: "The plurality of languages is far from reducible to a plurality of designations of a thing: they are different perspectives on this same thing, and when the thing is not the object of the external senses, we are dealing with so many things differently shaped by each and every one of us."[36] Each language is thus a net cast out into the world, which trawls other fish, and the diversity of languages becomes a "condition of the richness of the world and of the diversity of what we know about it; the realm of human existence is at the same thereby expanded for us, and new ways of thinking and feeling, with specific and real characteristics, are offered to us." In this regard, "Globish" represents a truly catastrophic scenario. All that it allows to remain alongside it are dialects—these dialects being French, German, and so on, but also the English of Shakespeare and of Joyce—that one uses to acquire new shares in the market.

Europe is right to commit actively to maintaining linguistic plurality. The fact that Jan Figel has as his title and remit "European commissioner responsible for culture and multilingualism" is a privilege we should not turn our noses up at.[37] Hannah Arendt, who practices this linguistic plurality on a daily basis in writing her *Denktagebuch* (Thought Diary), explains it as a philosophical gesture:

> Plurality of languages: If there were only one language, we would perhaps be more reassured about the essence of things.
>
> What is crucial is the fact 1) that there are many languages and that they differ not only in vocabulary, but also in grammar, and so in mode of thought, and 2) that all languages can be learned.
>
> . . . Within a homogenous human community, the essence of a table is indicated unambiguously by the word "table," and yet as soon as it reaches the borders of the community, it wavers.
>
> This wavering equivocation of the world and the insecurity of those who live in it would naturally not exist if it were not possible to learn foreign languages. . . . Whence the absurdity of universal language, which goes against the "human condition," and is an artificial and all powerful harmonization of this equivocation."[38]

It is because languages cannot be imposed interchangeably upon one another that equivocation is not reducible to contextual obscurity, but itself defines a "condition" that is meaningful and full of interest.

"Translate This Page"

Translation is the best touchstone. The difficulties of machine translation shine so many spotlights on what makes the singularity of languages. The stumbling block of translation is always, true to Arendt's diagnosis, of the order of homonymy, in syntactical as well as semantic terms. Indeed, multiplicity is not only apparent between languages, but also within each language. In other words, homonymy is what constitutes a language in its quintessence: "A language is, among others, the integral of the equivocations its history has allowed to persist"—what Jacques Lacan writes about the different "lalangues" of each unconscious is true of each and every language.[39] These homonymies appear in broad daylight whenever one wants to translate, that is, whenever one looks at one language from the perspective of another language.

"Translate this page," Google suggests obligingly. Machine translation is an immense construction site, and a philosophical reflection on the differences between natural languages can help us to understand it better. We could begin by pointing out how poor the actual result is, which stumbles, as anticipated, over homonymy. So, for example, in the results page for the founding article on Google's "Anatomy," it translates "novel research activities" into French as "*des activités de recherches de roman*" [activities involving searches for novels], and "novel research uses" as "*des utilisations de recherches de roman*" [usages involving searches for novels]. For a moment, I thought there was something to understand here.

I would like to share a fun little experiment I performed, starting out with a short sentence which contains an important part of the culture of the "Western world," and whose homonymic treachery is merely a sign of how vague its prepositions are. I entered the sentence "*Et Dieu créa l'homme à son image*" [And God created man in his image] into Google Translate, and asked it to translate into English, then asked for the French translation of the English sentence I got, then the English translation of the French sentence I got, and so on until I got a stable translation, with the same English sentence and the same French sentence. The difference makes one think about the difference between the two languages:

1. "*Et Dieu créa l'homme à son image*"
2. And God created the man with his image.

3. *Et Dieu a créé l'homme avec son image.*
4. And God created the man with his image.
5. *Et Dieu a créé l'homme avec son image.*

I did the same for French and German, starting out from the French, or from the German. Let us savor the point at which it becomes blasphemous, which is linked to the way in which it handles word order as well as the meaning and use of the article:

1. *"Et Dieu créa l'homme à son image"*
2. *Und Gott schuf den Menschen an seinem Bild.*
3. *Et a créé un dieu l'homme à son image*
4. *Und Einen Gott hat der Mensch and seinem Bild geschaffen.*
5. *Et l'homme à son image a créé un dieu*
6. *Und der Mensch an seinem Bild hat einen Gott geschaffen*
7. *Et l'homme à son image a créé un dieu* [And man created a god in his image]

1. *"Und Gott schuf den Menschen zu seinem Bilde"* (Standard Contemporary German Bible. Revised translation based on the translation by Luther)
2. *Et a créé un dieu l'homme à son image*
3. *Und einen Gott hat der Mensch an seinem Bild geschaffen*
4. *Et l'homme à son image a créé un dieu*
5. *Und der Mensch an seinem Bild hat einen Gott geschaffen*
6. *Et l'homme à son image a créé un dieu*

There is nothing exceptional about Google. Like most search engines, and most of its main users, starting with the European Community, it uses Systran, which is at the moment the most effective machine translator. The way it works is that everything goes through a single pivot language, English. English, as one singular natural language among others, is transformed so as to function first of all as a generic language, "Globish," and then as a kind of transitional artifact, "Technish."

In order to do this, English first of all has to be "disambiguated."

In this respect, is it worth comparing the disambiguation of "is" proposed by Wordnet (*the* dictionary that supports all automatic analysis and artificial intelligence applications) with that of *esti*, which Aristotle gives in his *Metaphysics* and *Categories*. Kant would have been perfectly justified in saying that the former was rhapsodic, with its thirteen nonhierarchized and partially overlapping senses, and with no intelligible sequence.[40] With the distinction between existence and copula, then, under the heading of the copula, the distinction between on the one hand substance, and on the other hand accident, which then unfolds according to the range of categorial questions (how, which, in relation to what, where, when . . .), Aristotle remains probably a worthy challenger to Wordnet.

Whatever the case then, translating, like reducing fractions, consists of taking languages back to a single, neutral conceptual language, with no qualities, and like an exchanger authorizing the passage from some other natural language: The difference between natural languages is by definition accidental and reducible. There is at present, to my knowledge, no other alternative procedure enabling one to move between natural languages without the "English" intermediary, thus directly taking into account its networks and homonymies. We have not yet modeled the know-how of a good translator.

Our books and our languages, to attempt another differential and multiple sense of the possessive, are two domains that are culturally resistant to Google.

THE MISSING DIMENSION

Google, just like America, posits itself and acts as if it were a champion of democracy. As far as the America of George Bush goes, everyone will find a way of making allowances. As for Google, one has to acknowledge the genius, closely linked to the Web, that consists in making a maximum amount of information freely available to a maximum number of people, and the genius, closely linked to the spirit of capitalism, which consists in earning money, a lot of money, with this "mission." The democratic claim of Google has, according to Google, two dimensions: an upstream democracy and a downstream democracy.

Upstream, each one of "us" makes up, in equal part or aristocratically weighted, a portion of the information that appears on the Web: "You are the Web," its content. Above all, everyone produces, in equal part and aristocratically weighted, the order of the information that the Web presents, in the same immanentist gesture: "You are the Web," its organization, this time via PageRank and the democracy of links and clicks.

Downstream, everyone has (or will/would have) free and equal access to the Web, in terms of the distribution of knowledge. And all of these aspects are connected, since the upstream of the link and the click produces the form that the downstream takes.

However, with respect to the idea of cultural democracy, we have to rethink both democracy and culture.

As far as culture goes, and this is really something of a statement of fact even if it is seldom acknowledged, the missing dimension is that of the artwork which, even open and "performed," is necessary for thinking languages as well as books. Once again culture cannot be reduced, any more than knowledge can, to the sum total of information—no more indeed than a sum total of pieces of information can make up information as such.

As far as democracy goes, that is another kettle of fish. What concept exactly of "democracy" is at stake here?

Here we can set to one side the flaws in the model, even if they are highly revealing. Tiananmen Square is symptomatic of the tension, even incompatibility, between a virtually realistic technical universal (everyone has or will have equal access, subject to digital fragmentation) and a globally unrealistic political universal (the Chinese, or other "nationals," do not and will not have the same access to identical content): A private politics is not the same as a public politics, and a public (state or national) politics is not the same as a global politics.

It is, I believe, the model itself that needs to be questioned, and we have to turn our attention to the very notion of democracy, of politics, and the status of the universal. In order to explain what to me does not seem democratic in Google's "democracy," I would like to take a good, long detour through Greece.

Google is a lot like sophistry. Throughout this book, I have constantly been struck by the traits they have in common. Now, the sophists are in my opinion, to use Hegel's expression, "the masters of Greece,"[41] the philosophers who taught him about both politics (democracy, to be precise) and culture. Yet Google seems to me far from being a master of politics or a master of culture. It is this contrastive comparison that I would now like to make in order to explain the relationship between Google and democracy.

Google is without doubt a Promethean kind of invention: cunning intelligence linked to simple and effective technical know-how that is also protean and quick to seize an opportunity. This complex description would be a great deal more eloquent in Greek. It would invoke terms (and these are sometimes words I have used in my own description along the way) like *mētis* ("scheme, astute scheme, astute and effective wisdom, ruse"), which characterizes the divine Ulysses, Zeus's plan, and the tentacular mobility of the octopus, *tekhnē* ("know-how, trade, technique, art, competence, expertise, way of doing, means, system, artifice"), *mēkhanē* ("means, discovery, ingenious invention, (war) machine, (theatrical) machinery, machination, expedient, thing, thingummy, talent, astuteness, art, resourcefulness"), *kairos* ("critical point, opportune or favorable moment, aptness, opportunity, advantage, profit"), and *kerdos* ("gain, profit, advantage, love of gain, profitable plans"). It would also draw on the language of rhetoric, in terms of *prepon* ("that which is distinguished, or presents or announces itself by its exterior aspect, what it appears as, and is related to and appropriate for what is most becoming, or adapted for an audience as well as for the subject being addressed"), and especially in terms of *doxa* ("opinion, reputation, appearance, semblance, belief"), *dokounta* ("appearances or judgments that seem to be appropriate, or are credible and around which a consensus can form"), or *endoxa* ("received ideas, established opinion, solid premises for likely reasoning").

Indeed, it is the world of sophistry that is being outlined here, subject as it is to the most extreme valorizations or devalorizations. In philosophy, Plato was the first to describe it as the "bad other": a pseudo-omnicompetence, with a grasp of the real and the everyday, but as far as possible from what truly counts, that is from the idea and from truth, and with a know-how that is concerned primarily with selling itself, and generating profit—a scandalous profit in the eyes of the Plato lying dormant in each and every one of us.

We might find ourselves, I might find myself, like Plato accusing sophist-Google of claiming to know everything, and diagnosing this claim of totalization as a symptom of the very inanity of this knowledge itself. We might reproach it, I might reproach it, for making available to anyone techniques that are catastrophic for knowledge and truth. To which Gorgias-Google would have no trouble replying, as he does in the *Gorgias* (Plato's *Gorgias*: Plato is still pulling the strings here), that it is not the teacher who is to blame, nor the technique he teaches his pupil, whether it is rhetoric or the art of combat, but the pupil himself when he misuses it: "It is the one who uses it incorrectly that it is right to hate, to send into exile, to kill, but not the one who teaches it" (457 c). Information is not harmful to truth; it is taking information for what it is not and using it wrongly that is harmful. The ball is in the user's court. Why on earth not use Google for what it is, and not for what it is not? All the information in the world is not claiming to be all the truth in the world—and just what is truth anyway?

We then come to a second line of attack, and a second line of defense, both philosophically more serious: The truth is what you have to look for, not all opinions are worth the same, there are true opinions, there are even truths as in mathematics, and "the Truth," as in philosophy. Plato's second criticism of sophist-Google might be that it only deals with opinions, and places all opinions on the same level: Protagoras, who claims that man is the measure of all things, would equally say, as a consistent relativist, that a pig or a baboon is the measure of all things. To which Protagoras has no trouble replying (in Plato's *Theaetetus*, in which Protagoras speaks through the mouth of Socrates, since it is again and still Plato who is pulling the strings): "Shame on you, Socrates!" And then arguing, as far as possible from the Truth contemplated then imposed by the philosopher-king on the indistinct crowd of those who cannot see clearly, that "a person has never been led from a false opinion to a true opinion." A doctor, a sophist, an orator, or a competent teacher, are on the other hand able "to lead someone from a less good state to a better state," and they are able to do it in such as way that "it is the things that are useful to society instead of harmful which seem right to them" (167 a–c). All opinions are not equivalent, which is why we need, politically and pedagogically, to make people capable of preferring that which is better (as a comparative, and not an absolute superlative), in other words what is better "for" (taking into consideration the contextualized singularity of the individual as well as of the society). Politics is not a matter of imposing the truth universally, or imposing a universal Truth—that would be "political philosophy," and a "professional deformation" of the philosopher, as Hannah Arendt would say, but it would not be politics. It consists of differentially helping to choose what is better. Indeed, with the sophistic reply it is the dimension of the political which makes its appearance, and a certain kind of politics that is at a remove from the universal, as well as the dimension of *paideia* (from *pais*, "child"), or "education" and "culture" as sharing a language, learning to read, exchanging speeches, the agonistics of persuasion, which some masters are of course better at teaching than others.

This is precisely the dimension that does not exist with Google, and which takes us to the limit of the comparison with sophistry. "Mass personalization" (what Salaün calls "the age old fantasy of marketing professionals") is not democracy. One plus one plus one does not make a community, nor an assembly, nor a *demos*,

a "people," nor moreover a "multitude" (a nomadic and differentiated anti-people), but a group of "idiots," in the strict sense of the
term, that is, private individuals (deprived of the public dimension),
reduced to their singularity as simple particulars, to their "proper"
dimension of unknown and ignorant people. And clicking is not
a political exercise of government (-*cracy*). There is no power at
stake or, more precisely, there is nothing, no intermediary body,
that enables it to be exercised. Believing that the sum of all singu-
lars makes up the universal, and more radically no doubt, believing
that it is about constituting the Universal, is a double equivalence
symptomatic of the elision or the omission of political. The resulting effect is the omission of the *paideia*, since the basis of this "apo-
litical democracy" is an equality between users whose knowledge is
unequal, so that someone ignorant weighs as much as a someone
knowledgeable in structuring what he does not know.

To put it brutally, Google is a champion of cultural democracy,
but without culture and without democracy, since it is a master neither of culture (information is not *paideia*) nor of politics (the democracy of clicks is not a democracy).

Just because Google elides the dimension of the political does
not mean that it does not exist politically, quite the opposite. One
could even say that Google is antidemocratic because it is profoundly American without giving us the means to know it, to question its universality, so that "American" has to be taken for granted as
universal. We are Aristotelian whenever we speak, whether we like
and know it or not; we are American whenever we Google, whether
we like and know it or not. One symptom of this is in my view
the terrible conclusion of John Battelle's otherwise good book *The
Search*. He is searching the term "immortality" (his youngest child
has just been born, and this is the word that occurs to him), and he
describes his search on Google. After a few uncomfortable wrong
turns of the "Immortality Institute" variety, he comes across an ad
for "Gilgamesh," which he does not buy, because he wants it right
away. Then, through a professor in Washington, he finds "the oldest

known human author we can call by his name," Shin-eqi-unninni, who, he say, "lives on in my mind." He then thinks of Ulysses, who prefers the immortality of fame to Calypso's life without death. "And does not search offer the same immortal imprint: is not existing forever in the indexes of Google and others the modern-day equivalent of carving our stories into stone? For anyone who has ever written his own name into a search box and anxiously awaited the results, I believe the answer is yes."[42] This is most distressing, not because it would be a collection of howlers but because it is the paradigm of an information culture as such, of the I Google (myself)/Google for myself (the middle voice in Greek), with the subjective and quasionanistic solitude of the long-distance googler. What we see here is the total absence of an intermediate reality: me/me/me, the World Wide Web and a search engine make up neither a shared, common world, nor sophistically arranged worlds. Yet the Web is an ongoing collective creation. It is even capable of producing spaces of confrontation, of *agōn* and *dissensus*, taking us beyond the capture of borders and war conflicts, as we saw recently with Lebanese and Israelis.[43] It is in this sense, both collective and performative, that it is politically eminently sensible. But instead of the political, with Google we find the transcendence of a disclaimer, a philosopher-king, except that it is not a philosopher—it is "the worst."

The immanence of the Web and the transcendence of Google: Is Google now the name of the transcendence of the Web?

Or rather, to put it more succinctly: *we, Google of America?*

Pino Marine, August 2006

NOTES

TRANSLATOR'S PREFACE

1. *Sophistical Practice: Towards a Consistent Relativism* (New York: Fordham University Press, 2014); *Jacques le Sophiste: Lacan, logos et psychoanalyse* (Paris: Epel, 2013; English translation forthcoming from Fordham University Press).

2. *Dictionary of Untranslatables: A Philosophical Lexicon*, ed. Barbara Cassin, Emily Apter, Jacques Lezra, and Michael Wood (Princeton: Princeton University Press, 2014). Originally published in French as *Vocabulaire européen des philosophies: Dictionnaire des intraduisibles* (Paris: Robert-Le Seuil, 2004).

3. Barbara Cassin, *Derrière les grilles: Sortons du tout-évaluation* (Paris: Mille et Une Nuits, 2014).

PREFACE TO THE ENGLISH-LANGUAGE EDITION

1. See Chapter 5.

2. "A word is so little the sign of a concept that the concept without the word cannot arise, nor could it even be held firm; the indeterminate action of the force of thought is condensed in the word just as soft clouds appear in a clear sky . . . Such a synonymy of main languages has never before been attempted, even though we find fragments of such attempts in many writers, but it would be, if it is done intelligently, a most seductive work." Wilhelm von Humboldt, *Essays on Language*, ed. T. Harden and D. Farrelly, trans. John Wieczorek and Ian Roe (New York: Peter Lang, 1997), 33–35.

3. Eric Schmidt and Jonathan Rosenberg, *How Google Works* (New York: Grand Central Publishing, 2014).

4. Gideon Lewis-Kraus, "The Great A.I. Awakening," *New York Times Magazine*, December 14, 2016.

5. Jorge Luis Borges, "El original es infiel a la traducción," from "Sobre el 'Vathek' de William Beckford," *Obras Completas* (Buenos Aires: Emecé Ediciones, 1989), 107–10.

6. For Protagoras, see for example Sextus Empiricus, *Outlines of Pyrrhonism*, I, 32, 216–219: "Man is the measure of all things [*pantōn khrēmatōn anthrōpos metron*], of things that are, that they are, of things that are not, that they are not." For Plato, see *Laws*, IV, 716 c–e: "God is for us the measure of all things" [*ho dē theos hēmin pantōn khrēmatōn metron eiē*]. For Aristotle, see the *Nicomachean Ethics*, IV, 1119 b 26: "We call *khrēmata* everything whose value is measured by money" [*khrēmata de legomen panta hosōn hē axia nomismati metreitai*].

INTRODUCTION: WHY BE INTERESTED IN GOOGLE?

1. Jacques Lacan, "L'Etourdit," *Scilicet* 4 (1973): 5–52, at 47.

2. Originally published in French as *Voir Hélène en toute femme: D'Homère à Lacan* (Paris: Editions Institut Synthelabo, 2000).

3. [Quaero—Latin for "I seek"—was the name given to the multimedia, multilingual European search engine developed with the goal of challenging the dominance of Google and American search engines generally. —Trans.]

4. ["Globish" and its assumption of English as an unquestioned meta-language become for Cassin a core focus and one of the principal targets of her Untranslatables project, which aims to decenter and displace its position of linguistic dominance globally. Many of the terms she references as examples of "Globish" in the present volume, such as *knowledge-based society*, are in English in the original French text, and where possible I have used italics to retain this mark of critical distance. —Trans.]

5. See John Battelle, *The Search: How Google and Its Rivals Rewrote the Rules of Business and Transformed Our Culture* (Boston: Nicholas Brealey, 2005), on which my discussion is to a large extent based. See also David A. Vise, *The Google Story* (New York: Delacorte, 2005), which is very well informed by more of a justification, and the critique of these two books by John Lanchester, *London Review of Books* 28, no. 2 (January 2006). See

also the site http://www.google-watch.org, which devotes itself to keeping a critical watchful eye on Google. [Google bought the rights from Stanford, for an estimated $337 million worth of shares, to have exclusive use of the PageRank licence. The patent is due to expire in 2017. Daniel Brandt, who set up and ran google-watch.org, took the site down in February 2012, apparently as a result of continuous denial-of-service attacks by hackers, rendering it unsustainable. —Trans.]

6. See Box A in Chapter 1.

7. Jean-Noël Jeanneney, *Quand Google défie l'Europe: Plaidoyer pour un sursaut* (Paris: Mille et Une Nuits, 2005). A second revised and expanded edition was published in September 2006. English translation by Teresa Lavender Fagan, *Google and the Myth of Universal Knowledge: A View from Europe* (Chicago: University of Chicago Press, 2007).

8. Galileo is the European satellite navigation system, GPS the American system. On the "disclaimer," see Box E.

1. THE INTERNET REVEALED THROUGH GOOGLE

1. This is the opening sentence of David Vise's book *The Google Story* (New York: Delacorte, 2005).

2. [*Les Guignols de l'Info* is a long-running satirical news program on French TV featuring latex puppet caricatures of well-known politicians and personalities. The reference is to a sketch from 1996 when Jacques Chirac, France's president at the time, was mocked for his ignorance about information technology. —Trans.]

3. This was what Terry Winograd, one of Larry Page's professors at Stanford, exclaimed in 1997 when Stanford licensed Google and made it accessible via google.stanford.edu (see Vise, *The Google Story*, 39).

4. I am quoting Page from the remarkable interview that the "Google Guys" gave to *Playboy* in September 2004.

5. I have chosen to include in several dialog boxes the digressions that have seemed to me necessary in order to understand better what Google is all about.

6. [Le Comte de Lautréamont, *Poésies II*. René Char, quoted in Maurice Blanchot, *The Infinite Conversation*. —Trans.]

7. "He is its organ, and it is his organ," is how Schleiermacher characterized the relationship between an author and his language.

8. See Box B, "Alexandria, Alex(andr)a, or Capitalism and Schizophrenia."

9. [As of October 2016, there are over 39 million articles, more than 5 million in English, and 1.7 million in French, in 292 languages. —Trans.]

10. I have used "free" twice here, meaning both copyright-free and with free, open content, to which anyone can add, as the reference to "copyleft" that appears in its features stipulates. On "copyleft," see Chapter 5.

11. See the *Financial Times* from December 19, 2005, in which Jimmy Wales responds to (or answers for—but does anything remain of responsibility in that sense?) the biography, published online, of someone who collaborated with former US Attorney General Robert Kennedy, in which he is accused of being implicated in the assassination of the two Kennedy brothers.

12. [*Bouvard et Pécuchet*, an unfinished work by Gustave Flaubert, published posthumously in 1881, tells the story of two copyeditors in Paris who become close friends, and who aim to explore every branch of human knowledge. All their efforts fail miserably, and they end up returning to "copying as before." —Trans.]

13. Or "plagiarizing and pasting," as Pascal Lardellier puts it (*"Google pillé-collé, l'arme fatale des étudiants"* [Google plagiarized and pasted, the students' deadly weapon], *Libération*, April 12, 2006).

2. GOOGLE INC.: FROM SEARCH TO GLOBAL CAPITAL

1. David A. Vise, *The Google Story* (New York: Delacorte, 2005), 39.

2. In "The Anatomy of a Large-Scale Hypertextual Web Search Engine," the inaugural description of Google (on the Stanford University website).

3. Neil Taylor, *Search Me: The Surprising Success of Google* (London: Cyanbooks, 2005), 63.

4. The *Oxford English Dictionary* defines "quark" as follows: "Physics: any of a group of subatomic particles which carry a fractional electronic electric charge and are believed to be building blocks of protons and other particles.

—ORIGIN invented by the American physicist Murray Gell-Mann and associated by him with the line 'Three quarks for Muster Mark' in James Joyce's *Finnegans Wake* (1939), which seemed appropriate because three kinds of quark were originally proposed." Not to mention, of course, the homonym "Quark"[2]: "A type of low-fat curd cheese."

—ORIGIN German, 'curd, curds.'"

5. See Box C.

6. I wish I were able to reproduce here some of these logos, which are so expressively opportunistic, such as the one from the soccer World Cup with its Os as two balls, but one can find them by googling "Google logos" and following the links (the most recent can be found on www.logo collect.com).

7. Vise, *The Google Story*, 275.

8. Their photographs are everywhere, and too expensive to reproduce here: like two still dreamy twins smiling at their triumph (see the illustrations of the *Anatomy* and those in the Playboy interview), or relaxing together in a hot tub, with their feet fanned out, in their Menlo Park office (see the photo section in Vise, *The Google Story*).

9. Sergey's great grandmother had gone to the University of Chicago to study microbiology, but she had chosen to return home in 1921 in order to be involved in building the Soviet state.

10. sergey, page@cs.stanford.edu. Google itself was accessible internally from 1997 on the site google.stanford.edu.

11. For this reason, Heidegger translates *logos* as "laying and gathering together," wondering "how *legein*, whose proper meaning is to 'lay out,' comes to mean saying and speaking," via *legen* (German) [to assemble, bring together], then *lesen* (German) [to read], but also "to gather, spread out," as well as "to glean, harvest, pick, store away, preserve, put inside" ("*Logos*" [Heraclitus, fragment 50]). One of the first meanings of *logos* was "proportion" in the mathematical sense of the term, and "relation," whence the double meaning of "reason" and "speech" (*ratio* and *oratio*, as it was translated into Latin).

12. These comments, made at a high school in Israel in September 2003, are cited by Vise in chapter 1 of *The Google Story*.

13. The "visible Web" is the public Web (the "www"), the one indexed by search engines, unlike the private Web (business "intranets," for example, and not "internets": see Box A), the content of hard drives, and the "intimate" Web of email, which makes up the "invisible Web." But the difference between the two is gradually disappearing: businesses are using

"corporate" search solutions internally (those sold by Google in particular), Gdesktop is indexing hard drives, Gmail is collecting and scanning e-mail, and the incomparable services offered by Google are only possible because of indexing. Hence the "big brother" effect I talk about later. "Blogs," which by definition confide private or intimate information to the public Web, make things even more confusing.

14. On Google's languages, see Chapter 5.

15. Another extraordinary word, since as well as a "blow" it is a "score" or a big "success," as in "hit parade." There are two types of "hit" for Google: "fancy hits" (URL addresses, titles, anchor texts for a link, or metatags) and "plain hits."

16. The game Google Whacks consists of finding a two-word query that generates a single answer from Google. More seriously, if you type "soup recipe for * and tomato," Google suggests basil and pumpkin for * (but when I try, it suggests the Wikipedia site where you can find this example), and you could widen it to include synonyms by typing a tilde before the item.

17. See Chapter 3.

18. *Bulletin Flaubert*, no. 77: see the article by Pierre Assouline in *Le Monde*, February 25, 2006.

19. [Eric Schmidt stepped down as CEO of Google in 2011. As of mid-2017, the CEO was Sundar Pichai, who assumed the post in 2015. —Trans.]

20. See Chapter 5.

21. Battelle, *The Search*, 294 n. 3. See the court cases—more than 110 between October 2004 and September 2005—listed on the site http://www.chillingeffects.org/international/keyword.cgi?KeywordID=60.

22. See the list of acquisitions and of services and tools, constantly being updated, given by Wikipedia under "Google" ("Acquisition and partnerships" and "Other products").

23. See Vise, *The Google Story*, 174–75, and all of chapter 16.

24. See Chapter 4.

25. [The share price in May 2017 was $958. —Trans.].

26. Quote in Vise, *The Google Story*, 255.

27. Main sources: Christophe Guillemin http://www.zdnzt.fr/actualités/Internet, accessed July 11, 2006; Wikipedia "Google," accessed July 11, 2006.

3. OUR MISSION IS TO ORGANIZE THE WORLD'S INFORMATION

1. For more on the deictic, see the section "Sense Certainty, or the This and Meaning of the This," in Hegel's *Phenomenology of Mind*, A,1.

2. "The trust of our people in God should be declared on our national coins," the secretary of the treasury, Salmon Chase, wrote in 1861, during the Civil War. The motto appeared for the first time in 1864 on the two-cent coin. It was not in fact used more widely until a law was voted on in the House of Representatives in 1956. No doubt it required nothing less than the "trust," or faith, in God in order to guarantee "trust" in money, in its trustworthiness, and the trustworthiness of the American economy, especially since "we" are no longer living under the gold standard regime, but rather the antitrust regime.

3. Speech delivered on September 12, 2001, following the meeting of the National Security Council.

4. Ibid.

5. Cited in David A. Vise, *The Google Story* (New York: Delacorte, 2005), 278.

6. George W. Bush, September 15, 2001, for this and the following quotation.

7. "Freedom and democracy are under attack" (September 12, 2001, speech): "Today, our fellow citizens, our way of life, our very freedom came under attack" (September 20, 2001, speech to joint session of Congress). One sentence cannot be superimposed on the other, and the "we" ("our way of life") has nothing universal about it.

8. I am using "moral" here in the modern, that is, Kantian, sense of the term, defined by the universality of moral law, and the direct relation between the individual "in me" and the universal "all without exception." This is contrasted to the ethical (from *ēthos*, habit, custom, related to *ēthos*, "character") in an Aristotelian sense, explicitly defined in relation to the norms of a community and to the prudence of judgment. On might characterize the "relativism" of the modern age by the way in which Nietzsche, "beyond good and evil," unmasks the so-called universality of values as determined by the interests of a particular sector, relative to a community and its domination, and deeply inscribed and embedded through education and language.

9. Victor Klemperer, *Language of the Third Reich: LTI, Lingua Tertii*

Imperii—A Philologist's Notebook, English translation by Martin Brady
(London: Bloomsbury, 2006):

> LTI: *Lingua Tertii Imperii*, the language of the Third Reich. Many a time
> I have been reminded of an old Berlin anecdote . . . "Father," a young
> boy asks in the circus, "what is the man up there on the tightrope doing
> with that pole?"—"Silly boy, it's a balancing pole, and it's what's holding
> him steady."—"Oh dear, father, what if he lets go of it?"—"Silly boy, he's
> holding it steady, of course!"
>
> Again and again during these years my diary was my balancing pole,
> without which I would have fallen down a hundred times . . . at all these
> times I was invariably helped by the demand that I had made on myself:
> observe, study and memorize what is going on—by tomorrow everything
> will already look different, by tomorrow evening everything will already
> feel different; keep hold of how things reveal themselves at this very
> moment and what the effects are. And very soon this call to rise above the
> situation and to safeguard my inner freedom was concentrated into that
> consistently effective secret formula: LTI, LTI" (9–10).

Subsequent references are abbreviated to LTI and immediately follow
quotations in text.

10. Brin, in the interview in *Playboy*, September 2004.

11. [In French in the original. —Trans.]

12. "New Year Address," January 2006.

13. This is at any rate the information that Google provides on its own
site, under "Technology."

14. Several articles provide an explanation for mathematicians of how
this Markov chain works, for example, Amy Langville and Karl Meyer,
"Deeper Inside PageRank" (October 2004, on the Internet), or Ian Rogers,
"The Google PageRank Algorithm and How It Works."

15. "The Anatomy of a Large-Scale Hypertextual Web Search Engine,"
Sergey Brin and Lawrence Page. Henceforth abbreviated as "Anatomy." See
the presentation of the initial algorithm in "Anatomy," so simple that it
could be calculated within a few hours for 26 million pages on an average
computer:

> We assume page A has pages T1 . . . Tn which point to it (i.e., are
> citations). The parameter d is a damping factor which can be set

between 0 and 1. We usually set d to 0.85. There are more details about d in the next section. Also C(A) is defined as the number of links going out of page A. The PageRank of a page A is given as follows:

$$PR(A) = (1-d) + d(PR(T1)/C(T1) + \ldots + PR(Tn)/C(Tn))$$

Note that the PageRanks form a probability distribution over web pages, so the sum of all PageRanks will be one.

The actual algorithm integrates variables enabling the detection of spam, and of "trick clicks" designed to distort the ranking.

16. Vise, *The Google Story*, 38.

17. The site of all sites, in other words Google, is itself included in Google, whereas Alta Vista was not included in Alta Vista.

18. Quoted by John Battelle in *The Search: How Google and Its Rivals Rewrote the Rules of Business and Transformed Our Culture* (Boston: Nicholas Brealey, 2005), 292 n. 4.

19. [Attention to rankings in National and World league tables is of course now integral to the reputation of Universities globally, and institutions do all they can to improve their ranking. The Shanghai Index, or Academic Ranking of World Universities, is primarily focused on the Sciences and Social Sciences. Efforts are clearly paying off for French universities: in 2015, Paris Vi was ranked 36, Paris XI 41, the ENS 72 and Strasbourg 87. —Trans.]

20. This is the full set of the criteria used in calculating the Shanghai Index: the number of Nobel Prize winners in physics, chemistry, medicine, and economics; the number of Field medals; the number of most-cited researchers in twenty one scientific fields; the number of articles published in *Sciences* and *Nature*; the number of publications in the Science Quotation Index (sciences and social sciences)—where we find the Garfield Impact Factor again—and the "university performance" of each institution, themselves corresponding to quantifiable criteria.

21. I am borrowing these expressions from Romain Laufer, describing the "crisis of legitimacy." Once again, the researcher in the CNRS is constantly faced with this kind of evaluation: How many articles have you published in peer-reviewed journals in the last five years? Books are considered "off piste," and adding them to one's publication record is materially impossible.

22. "Why Google?"

23. See Box D.

24. "Why Google?"

25. See "Google and states," Chapter 4.

26. Likewise, from the perspective of intellectual property, Google's practice in the name of "fair use" is no longer "everything which is not explicitly authorized by the copyright holders is forbidden," but "everything which is not explicitly forbidden is authorized." The publisher La Martinière/Le Seuil took Google to court to protest against this wrong use of "fair use." The case is ongoing. See Chapter 5.

27. See, for example, the story about 2bigfeet.com.

28. The strange caesura of this word is worth noting, and what is more, it is badly formed in that it mixes Latin and Greek; unlike auto/matic, it should be *informa/tique*—but whatever the case may be, it is "clear"!

29. Cybernetics is another keyword that has come to French from English, *kubernētikē technē*, the art of governing or steering, from pilots to heads of state, according to the analogy already operative in Plato's *Politics*. Ampère had already Gallicized the Greek term in 1834 in his *Essai sur la philosophie des sciences* [Essay on the Philosophy of Science], in the Platonic sense of 'science of governing men," but without being taken any further.

30. *The Human Use of Human Beings: Cybernetics and Society* (New York: Da Capo, 1954), 17–18.

31. Battelle puts forward the hypothesis that if journalists like Google so much (without any advertising budget, it has become famous thanks to word of mouth, but also thanks to journalists), it is because it helps them to do their job (294 n. 8), thereby further confirming that it is about information.

32. Interview, *Playboy*, September 2004.

33. [The strategic goal for 2020, following the global economic crisis of 2008, now reads: "The Europe 2020 strategy is about delivering growth that is: *smart*, through more effective investments in education, research and innovation; *sustainable*, thanks to a decisive move towards a low-carbon economy; and *inclusive*, with a strong emphasis on job creation and poverty reduction. The strategy is focused on five ambitious goals in the areas of employment, innovation, education, poverty reduction and climate/energy." As part of this, the "Digital Agenda" reads as follows: "Creating a

single digital market based on fast/ultrafast internet and interoperable applications" —Trans.]

34. Article for the journal *Regard sur l'actualité*, December 2005. *La Documentation française* (10 n. 26 in the version of October 20, 2005). The article can be found online at http://archivesic.ccsd.cnrs.fr/docs/00/06/26/68/RTF/sic_00001576.rtf.

35. See, however, the way in which UNESCO's charter on cultural diversity very carefully constructs the notion of "cultural expression."

36. "The Crisis in Culture," in *Between Past and Future: Eight Exercises in Political Thought* (Harmondsworth, UK: Penguin Books, 1968), 210. Henceforth abbreviated to CC, with page references immediately following quotation in parentheses.

37. Or what Pierre Lévy calls "collective intelligence" ("L'intelligence collective et ses objets," 1994, on the Web, and see more recently his *Cyberdémocratie* [Paris: Odile Jacob, 2002]). By contrast, Wikipedia notes under "cyberculture," referring to its "principal theorist," that the term designates "precisely what Wikipedia is an example of." The generous interpretation would thus be to consider Wikipedia as performative as much as it is informative.

4. DON'T BE EVIL

1. The full title of this interview, which I have already cited frequently, is "Google Guys: A candid conversation with America's newest billionaires about their oddball company, how they tamed the Web and why their motto is 'Don't be evil.'" This is the interview *Playboy* published in September 2004, during the reserve period just before the company's IPO, and the timing meant it had to be appended to the Securities and Exchange Commission file [see Chapter 2], although it is not easy to know if they were throwing a "googly" in publishing this interview. For my part, I have to give the "Google Guys" credit for demonstrating such supreme mastery and irony in getting *Playboy* into the SEC!

2. "Conditions of use—Changes to terms and conditions of Google search services" (my emphasis).

3. See Chapter 2.

4. David A. Vise, *The Google Story* (New York: Delacorte, 2005), 115, as well as all of chapter 10.

5. See "AdWord" and "AdSense" on the Google website. AdSense generated 15 percent of Google's revenue in 2005. See John Battelle, *The Search: How Google and Its Rivals Rewrote the Rules of Business and Transformed Our Culture* (Boston: Nicholas Brealey, 2005), 152.

6. As discussed in the Introduction.

7. "Why Google?" (my emphasis).

8. However, "The Quality Score is determined by your keyword's click-through rate (CTR), relevance of your ad text, historical keyword performance, and other relevancy factors specific to your account" (under "Evaluating Your Keyword Performance").

9. Vise, *The Google Story*, 90; Battelle, *The Search*, 166.

10. http://google.com/adwords. [Current information about AdWords on Google's website no longer links them to their general mission. —Trans.].

11. Interview in *Playboy*. As Paul Ford writes, in "The Banality of Google" (September 2004, http://www.ftrain.com/GoogleP.html): "Because Google can be trusted. Google's unofficial slogan is 'Don't be evil,' and you can totally trust that. I mean, even Hannah Arendt (1906–1975) bought stock in Google! She totally did."

12. "PageRank is a champion of democracy," in "Why Google?" See Chapters 3 and 5.

13. http://google.com/adwords.

14. Snap.com, unlike Google, does not charge per click, but only when the click is followed by some action (that is not necessarily a purchase).

15. A sample passage gives a flavor of this: "Detection and filtering techniques: each click on an AdWords ad is examined by our system. A lot of information is checked by Google for each click, particularly the IP address, the time of the click, double clicks, and other parameters. This information is used to identify and filter potentially invalid clicks. We cannot divulge detailed information on our practices, but we can assure you that we are working constantly to develop and improve the software used. The Google Team: In parallel with our automated techniques for protection against invalid clicks, our team uses specialized techniques and tools to study specific cases of invalid clicks. When our system detects potentially invalid clicks, a technician examines the corresponding account in order to collect important data on the source of these clicks."

16. See, for example, Google on Wikipedia, and the doubts expressed

by Olivier Andrieu, a specialist in PageRanking, in his blog Abondance.com (May 31, 2006).

17. It is true that this bomb is a fake, that is to say, a false page imitating Google but not produced by Google, and which clever activists have managed to get ranked first. I am not sure that the user could tell the difference.

18. Battelle, *The Search*, 159.

19. "Terms of Service—Content used by Google."

20. See Box E.

21. See Chapter 5.

22. Part II. Other information: Item 1. Legal proceedings.

23. Internet Explorer, the Windows operating system, violated antitrust law.

24. These are Tim Berners-Lee's expressions in his founding articles "Semantic Web Road Map" (http://www.w3.org/DesignIssues/Semantic.html .septembre 1998) and "Semantic Web," with James Hendler and Ora Lassila (ScientificAmerican.com, May 2001). It is easy to see why the Semantic Web (which experts consider moreover either as an ideal, or a joke), as a form of "artificial intelligence," should enthuse a historian of classical philosophy who is familiar with, first and foremost, Aristotle, the Stoics, and Leibniz: it offers (1) a representation of knowledge, (2) with the help of a language of the predicate/category type, (3) that determines one or more "ontologies," used to define formally classes of objects and the relations between them.

25. This can be consulted on the website http://www.ftrain.com/google _takes_all.html. This article opens with a drawing of the little robot "Googlebot" walking, with the caption: "I am Googlebot. I control the earth," which Google wanted to reproduce on its corporate T-shirts. See Battelle, *The Search*, 263–266. The extraordinary Webfountain Project, created by IBM, which refilters the Web at your request in a few days, at a considerable cost, is already a semantic application.

26. See Chapter 2.

27. [This is now "Google Shopping." —Trans.]

28. About ten minutes ago I clicked on Gmail and—"Don't throw anything away"—the amount of megabytes available to me kept growing on the homepage. The size of the accounts increases by about 4 bytes per second.

29. We can see from Sergey Brin's homepage at Stanford that he was already aware of this in 1998.

30. *The Onion*, a satirical newspaper distributed for free in some American cities, ran a story on August 31, 2005, with the headline: "Google Announces Plan to Destroy All Information It Can't Index." GooglePurge, via DeskTop, was going to wipe the content of hard disks and books it had not indexed, while an army of robots scanned the gene pool of a hundred humans a day. So Google's slogan would certainly have been expanded to: "Don't be evil unless it's necessary for the greater good."

31. See Chapter 3, and for the problem of copyright, Chapter 5.

32. See Chapter 5.

33. For example, free and open access to a considerable memory, permanent archiving, the possibility of grouping messages and replies together in a single conversation, automatic filtering that recognizes spam, search and chat function since February 2006.

34. I quote from the version published on October 14, 2005.

35. See Chapter 3.

36. Vise, *The Google Story*, chapter 26. John Craig Venter, a biologist and businessman, according to Wikipedia, founded Celera Genomics and launched the Human Genome Project. This time it is "all the genes on the planet" (for now, 30,000 of them) that he plans to map out, according to the National Institute of Health.

37. "The right of the people to be secure in their persons, houses, papers, and effects, against unreasonable searches and seizures, shall not be violated." See the excellent analysis by Battelle, *The Search*, 197–204, and the whole of chapter 8, where he explains for example how the city of New York, taking into consideration the mix of its immigrant population and of students, and the compatibility between safety and freedom ("Americans can be both safe and free"), took the decision to refuse certain requests from the federal authorities.

38. See *Le Monde*, January 23, 2006.

39. Sources: abundance.com and infos-du-net.com.

5. ON CULTURAL DEMOCRACY

1. See David A. Vise, *The Google Story* (New York: Delacorte, 2005), chapter 21. See also "Google Book Search: News and Views" on the Google website, and the very detailed chronology offering numerous links on http://formats-ouverts.org/blog/2005/09/15/536-dossier-bibliotheque

-numerique-europeene. Finally, I recommend the article by Jean-Michel Salaün, "Bibliothèques numériques et Google Print," quoted earlier.

2. Many English language publishers and some publishers from other European countries signed an agreement, among them Editions de l'Eclat from France. Michel Valensi had for a long time been unconditionally committed to digital publishing, with his orthographical invention of "Lyber": "LYBER: masculine noun, 21st century, formed from the Latin word *liber*, which has several different meanings: free, book, child, wine (It is also the name of a God associated with Dionysus, whose feast day (Liberalia) is 17 March (the publication date of the book *Libres enfants du savoir numérique* [Free children of the world of digital knowledge]), and who has the distinction of not having his own temple!)." The "y" indicates that the concept belongs to the "Cyber" universe. English, however, prefers the word "Frook," a contraction of Free Book. (See "Petit traité plié en dix sur le Lyber," http://www.eclat.net/lyber/lybertext.html.) This agreement with Google—which the "Landernau" of French publishing was very excited about, as he says in his article "Faut-il une grande cuillère pour signer avec Google? [Do you need a big spoon to sign with Google?]—was signed on August 25, 2005.

3. The number was 50,000 according to Andreas von Bubnoff, in "The Real Death of Print," *Nature* 438 (December 2005), who goes on to give a numerical comparison. Superstar Reader, a Chinese company, had apparently already scanned 100,000 books, all Chinese. [As of 2016, Project Gutenberg offered more than 53,000 free e-books. —Trans.]

4. [According to the most recent data available, the number of volumes available has grown to well over 3 million, with 550,000 as text. —Trans.]

5. "La Bibliothèque numérique européenne, une stratégie culturelle du Web, Livre blanc: Les travaux du Comité de pilotage pour la bibliothèque numérique européenne" (July–December 2005). See also the "Résumé du Livre blanc du Comité de pilotage pour une bibliothèque numérique européenne," by Valérie Tesnière (January 2006).

6. See Box B. The article in *Nature* gave twelve online books for the Open Content Alliance in December 2005, but the initiative now brings together, around the simple logic of a digital warehouse with free content and open access, archive centers, publishers, and IT and Internet companies (such as Hewlett Packard and Adobe). MSN-Microsoft has also just joined.

7. The plan included a bilingual "Collaborative Digital Library," with

partners such as the Bibliothèque Nationale de France responsible for specific targeted projects (e.g. "France in America/*La France en Amérique*"). We might add that in October 2006 Cornell signed with Microsoft, while the University of California, the University of Wisconsin Madison, and the Complutense de Madrid joined the ranks of Google Book Search.

8. The main difference between "*droits d'auteur*" [author's rights] and copyright is the following: copyright only refers to the cultural heritage part of an author's rights that are linked to the work (representation, reproduction, reuse, and so on), but not to the "moral rights" linked to the person of the author (attribution, respect for the integrity of the work, right of withdrawal, and so on), which are nontransferable, perpetual, imprescriptible, and transmissible to the heirs or the executors of the will.

9. "Google Book Search: News and Views." For more on this controversy, see the analyses of the American Library Association, "The Google Library Project: The Copyright Debate" by Jonathan Band (January 2006), as well as the report by Robin Jeweler, legislative attorney for the American Law Division, "CRS Report for Congress. The Google Book Search Project: Is Online Indexing a Fair Use Under Copyright Law?" The question of fair use is linked to the current practice of peer-to-peer copying for personal use (particularly in the audio domain), the rules and regulations of which have seen many twists and turns in European law, and in French law in particular.

10. See Chapter 3.

11. "Fair use" is defined in section 107 of Title 17 of the United States Constitution. Google draws upon the precedent of *Kelly v. Arriba Soft Corp*: Arriba had given access to photos of Kelly in the form of thumbnails, which were also linked to the website of origin, and this was judged to be fair use.

12. [It is worth noting in passing that there is no equivalent of fair use in French law. —Trans.]

13. See Chapter 3.

14. [This is the definition Cassin gives of "Untranslatable" in her preface to the *Dictionary of Untranslatables*. —Trans.]

15. *Journal officiel* 143, 22 June 2004, Law no. 2004-575, 21 June 2004, on confidence in the digital economy, and which offers this definition of the equivalent French terms, *standard ouvert* (reference NOR:ECOX0200175L), article 4.

NOTES TO PAGES 100–105

16. François Stasse, in his report to the Minister of Culture and Communication "on access to digitized works kept in public libraries" (April 2005) shows how the constraints of on site consultation established by the European directive of May 22, 2001, mean a "neutralization of one of the main features of the digital revolution, namely the elimination of the distance between the work and the reader," and he is alarmed by the increasing imbalance in e-learning on the two sides of the Atlantic, which he sees as damaging to the spread of European cultures. It is disarming that everyone understands the direction in which "history" is traveling, but that it is so hard to follow it.

17. Yann Moulier-Boutang, "Richesse, propriété, liberté et revenue dans le 'capitalisme cognitif,' " *Multitudes* 5 (May 2001): 19. On the whole range of European directives concerning copyright and intellectual property, see Philippe Agrain, *Cause commune: L'information entre bien commun et propriété* (Paris: Fayard, 2005), in particular chapter 3. One cannot overlook the fact that the reporter of the directive on intellectual property at the European parliament in 2003 was Madame Fourtou, wife of Jean-René Fourtou, CEO of Vivendi-Universal, and President of the International Chamber of Commerce (see Aigrain, 22 and 143).

18. See Vise, *The Google Story*, 225 ff.

19. I hardly dare admit that "print media" means nothing to me. What counts is this copy of this edition, underlined, spoiled, annotated, and shelved next to this other book, bearing all the visual and tactile traces of using it over the years, which an electronic edition could never replace, whatever new possibilities it may open up.

20. Since the decision of the Conseil Constitutionnel in August 2006, on the grounds of equality in terms of penal law, users of peer-to-peer software in France can once again be sentenced to three years imprisonment and a fine of up to 300,000 euros if found guilty of piracy. [Against a background of ongoing debates around legal issues in relation to digital rights, no one to date has been prosecuted. —Trans.]

21. [Quaero ceased to exist in 2014, unable to resist the pressures of competition. —Trans.]

22. [This is the term Jeanneney uses (*tête de gondole* in the original French) in his *Google and the Myth of Universal Knowledge* to describe Google's hierarchizing and ranking of books. —Trans.]

23. Jean-Michael Salaün, in *Journal du CNRS* 188 (September 2005),

proposes that France and Europe direct their efforts not toward the construction of a European Google, but toward setting up an independent observer and a regulatory authority.

24. This is the fundamental point where I part company with the analyses of the "White Paper."

25. Maurice Godelier, who was involved with the European program ECHO (European Cultural Heritage Online), began by digitizing the heritage of the Tungusic people, in eastern Siberia. This gesture can still be considered something of a manifesto.

26. [This is nonsensical in French translation, and equally so in English, starting with the translation of "broadband" as *large bande*. —Trans.]

27. Battelle, *The Search*, 252.

28. See Box A.

29. François Bourdoncle is the CEO and cofounder of the Exalead Company. He was involved in developing the technology for the AOL search engine, and worked on Altavista's "refine" function. In 2005 he received the "Entrepreneur" prize from Thierry Breton. An interview with him, which I quote from, is available on http://www.agoravox.fr/article.php3?id_article=8641.

30. I am borrowing this term from Jean-Paul Nerrière, *Don't speak English. Parlez Globish*, 2nd rev. ed., (Paris: Eyrolles, 2006), although I do not share his conviction that the promotion of "Globish" allows us to safeguard French as a language of culture.

31. "E-mail to our friends," quoted in Vise, *The Google Story*, 97.

32. TöGEthé®
SINCE 1957

The "international" European logo designed to celebrate fifty years of the EU in 2007 is a glaring example of this triumph of Globish that multilingualism has to counteract! One might point out how closely it echoes Google's logo and materializes its *flavors* (with the umlaut and the acute accent), like spelling mistakes infecting this single language, and all placed under the aegis of global commercialization, with Europe as a brand to be franchised (see my article in *Le Monde*, November 3, 2006).

33. D'Alembert, Jean Le Rond, "Preliminary Discourse," in *The Encyclopedia of Diderot & d'Alembert Collaborative Translation Project*, translated by Richard N. Schwab and Walter E. Rex (Ann Arbor: University of Michigan Library, 2009); http://hdl.handle.net/2027/spo.did2222.0001.083

(accessed 20 December 2015). Originally published as "Discours Préliminaire," *Encyclopédie ou Dictionnaire raisonné des sciences, des arts et des métiers*, 1:i–xlv (Paris, 1751).

34. This is the one we have put into practice in the *Vocabulaire européen des philosophies: Des intraduisibles* (Paris: Editions du Seuil, 2004; English translation, *Dictionary of Untranslatables: A Philosophical Lexicon*, edited by Barbara Cassin, Emily Apter, Jacques Lezra, and Michael Wood (Princeton: Princeton University Press, 2014)), and which I have attempted to thematize in the Preface to this work. I refer the interested reader to this Preface.

35. Wilhelm von Humboldt, *Über die Verschiedenheiten des menschlichen Sprachbaues, in Gesammelte Schriften*, 7 vols., ed. A. Leitzmann et al. (Berlin: Behr, 1903–18), 6:240. English translation, Peter Heath, *On Language: On the Diversity of Human Language Construction and Its Influence on the Mental Development of the Human Species*, 2nd rev. ed. (Cambridge: Cambridge University Press, 1999).

36. Wilhelm von Humboldt, "Fragment de monographie sur les Basques" (1822), French translation by Pierre Caussat, Dariusz Adamski, and Marc Crépon in *La Langue source de la nation* (Paris: Madaga, 1996), 433, for this and the following quotation.

37. In November 2006 Leonard Orban was appointed to be responsible solely for multilingualism. [This post has undergone several changes since then, and it is now part of the Education, Culture, Multilingualism and Youth portfolio, a post held since 2014 by Tibor Navracsics under the Juncker Commission. —Trans.]

38. Hannah Arendt, *Denktagebuch*, Book 2.

39. Jacques Lacan, "L'Etourdit," *Scilicet* 4 (1973): 47. [Cassin draws out at much greater length the connection between Lacanian psychoanalysis, language, and sophistry in her book *Jacques le Sophiste: Lacan, Logos, et psychanalyse* (Paris: Epel, 2012). English translation forthcoming from Fordham University Press. —Trans.]

40. We thus find the copula in 1, identity in 2 (but again in 6 and 8), and existence in 4, while place is between the two in 3, and on the same level, very specific meanings (9, "to incarnate," as in "Derek Jacobi was Hamlet"), or very idiomatic meanings (10, "to spend or take time," as in "I may be an hour"), not to mention autonomous meanings that almost do not appear as such.

41. G. W. F. Hegel, *Lessons on the Philosophy of History*, trans. J. Sibree (Kitchener, Ontario: Bartoche Books, 287). For a more general discussion of the question, see Barbara Cassin, *L'effet sophistique* (Paris: Gallimard, 1995).

42. These are the final lines of the book, 284.

43. [Examples abound of how digital communication, and exploitation of the Web and of social media, have been an increasing aspect of political dissent since 2006 (e.g., the Arab Spring around 2010–12, terrorist groups in the Middle East and Africa, election campaigns in the West, leaks of formerly confidential political and financial data such as the Panama Papers, and so on). —Trans.]

INDEX

MEANING SYSTEMS

MEANING SYSTEMS

Bruce Clarke and Henry Sussman, series editors

Heinz von Foerster, *The Beginning of Heaven and Earth Has No Name: Seven Days with Second-Order Cybernetics*. Edited by Albert Müller and Karl H. Müller. Translated by Elinor Rooks and Michael Kasenbacher.

Bernhard Siegert, *Cultural Techniques: Grids, Filters, Doors, and Other Articulations of the Real*. Translated by Geoffrey Winthrop-Young.

Kriti Sharma, *Interdependence: Biology and Beyond.*

Bruce Clarke (ed.), *Earth, Life, and System: Evolution and Ecology on a Gaian Planet.*

Peter Harries-Jones, *Upside-Down Gods and Gregory Bateson's World of Difference.*

Jeffrey Champlin and Antje Pfannkuchen (eds.), *The Technological Introject: Friedrich Kittler between Implementation and the Incalcuable.*

Barbara Cassin, *Google Me: One-Click Democracy*. Translated by Michael Syrotinski.